Fashion Trend Forecasting

Gwyneth Holland
Rae Jones

Fashion Trend Forecasting

Laurence King Publishing

Published in Great Britain in 2017
Laurence King Student & Professional
An imprint of Quercus Editions Ltd
Carmelite House
50 Victoria Embankment
London EC4Y 0DZ

An Hachette UK company

Reprinted in 2021

A CIP catalogue record for this book is available
from the British Library

TPB ISBN 978-1-78627-058-0

10 9 8 7 6 5

Design: Charlotte Klingholz
Picture research: Giulia Hetherington

Image on page 2: Seasonal colour trend illustration by Unique Style Platform

Printed and bound in the UK by CPI Group (UK) Ltd, Croydon, CR0 4YY

Contents

Introduction

Trend forecasting in the fashion industry is a widely used but little understood skill, which aims to map a path between what consumers are doing and wearing now and what they might want to do and wear in the next few months and years.

Fashion forecasting exists to help predict what products brands and retailers should design and sell, minimizing risk and helping to prevent wasted effort and expenditure. It's also a way to keep one or two steps ahead of your target consumer; understanding them so that you can offer them useful and exciting fashion, and thereby gain their loyalty.

In this book we will demonstrate how to forecast fashion trends. We will look at how to produce a well-researched trend: taking inspiration, research and a clear and effective flow of information and translating that into a trend.

A trend forecaster needs to sense the moment when ideas from the fringes of culture are taken on by the mainstream consumer, then give an indication of where they think that will lead. Forecasters must watch constantly how the zeitgeist is changing and how this might affect their consumer, and therefore the kind of products they will want.

We aim to guide you through the processes needed to tap into the zeitgeist and give guidelines for training your instincts and formulating ideas, as well as how to track the evolution of a trend from inspiration to real product. It is important to remember that a forecast is not the same as a prediction, and it is difficult to be precise when gazing into the future, but any forecast you create should help to shape the future direction of your design, product development and brand image.

The ability to spot trends is now necessary at every level of fashion and lifestyle businesses, from sourcing, sales and operations to buying and merchandising, design and marketing.

Throughout this book, we will guide you through the key skills and practices needed to create a trend forecast, or even to become a trend forecaster. We have interviewed a selection of professionals from different aspects of the trends industry, looking at the path they took to get to where they are, and how they use trends within their daily life. We draw on years of experience as practising forecasters, as well as the expertise and experience of some of the industry's leading lights, to help you learn the art and science of trends.

Fabric swatches of seasonal colour trends.

1

Fashion Trends Then and Now

This chapter looks at the past, present and future of trends. It begins by examining how trends have developed across different eras, focusing on some of the key influences, their development and progression. The chapter concludes with the development of the trend industry, from its origins a century ago to its current and future prospects.

Trends have been around for many years – some academics date the beginning of trends to the fifteenth century. Since then, they have been informed by different individuals and groups, and shaped by external factors such as technology and politics.

For centuries, the progression in styles of dress was driven by changes in the ruling classes; new monarchies and political powers establishing themselves, for example. In relatively peaceful times, fashions could stay the same for decades.

Today, trends are most heavily influenced by fashion professionals and by consumers' own lifestyles. What we think of as beautiful, luxurious, comfortable or innovative is largely influenced by our lifestyles, and this will affect how fashion is created and worn. Now, thanks to the instant and global access to information online, we are more exposed than ever to changes in design, lifestyle and power – and to a more diverse range of influences, meaning that trends can now change quickly.

French fashion plate, 1825.

Historical view

There have always been trendsetters – people with innovative or distinctive ways of dressing that others want to emulate. Here, we look at how different roles have set trends in their style of dress and choice of lifestyle. The key realms of fashion influence throughout history have been the military, royalty, celebrities and fashion professionals such as designers and stylists. The term 'trend' was not used before the twentieth century to refer to changes in fashion, or the spreading of a particular style; styles that were created by these influencers were referred to as 'fashions' or 'modes'. In the following pages, we detail how and why these realms have influenced trends for centuries – and how they continue to do so.

Military influence

As a symbol of bravery, patriotism, hard work and function, military clothing has long influenced trends. Elements of military apparel are often adopted into everyday dress as a way of associating oneself with successful military campaigns or dashing conquerors, but have also been co-opted as a way to critique unpopular military campaigns.

One example of the military influencing fashion trends is the cravat. Originally a brightly coloured scarf worn around the necks of Croatian mercenaries serving in the French Army during the Thirty Years War of 1618–1648, it became hugely popular in France in the following decades, and became a key part of both court and everyday dress.

Military-inspired trends have often developed as a way to show allegiance to those in power, such as the uniforms adorned with braids and buttons worn in support of the French emperor, and general, Napoleon I.

During times of war or conflict, fashion trends have also adopted elements of military design to show support for those in battle, from Nelsoniana – accessories, homewares and clothing inspired by Lord Nelson's victories – to the motifs of the army, navy and air force that were adopted into civilian dress during World War II. The results were Utility dress styles in the UK and those influenced by similar legislation in the US and other countries. These styles echoed the strong shoulders and clean lines of the era's military uniforms, along with navy-style striped trims and sailor collars.

Until the mid-twentieth century, British and German royal children were dressed in sailor suits to associate them with their countries' successful navies, impacting childrenswear designs for decades. Military styles are continually being adapted to create new fashion trends, as a way to demonstrate toughness, practicality or officer-style panache.

Clockwise from top: Musician Jimi Hendrix on stage in his iconic hussar jacket; Camouflage is a popular military design, worn to suggest toughness and even rebellion, here by a member of the Manic Street Preachers; Sailor suits were commonly worn by royal children, and were emulated by children across the realm. These are the future kings George VI (left) and Edward VIII (right) in 1900.

Royal influence

The ruling classes have long had an influence on fashion and the spreading of trends. For many centuries, monarchies not only had total power, but were one of the most visible groups in society. In an age before photographs and mass media, people might not know what their king, queen or emperor looked like but could recognize them from the opulence of their dress alone. In this way, monarchs and royal families expressed their elite status and their difference from the rest of society.

Until the eighteenth century, many fashion trends across Europe, Africa and Asia could be traced back to royalty. Henry VIII (1491–1547), described as 'the best-dressed sovereign in the world' during his reign, created trends for voluminous and slashed sleeves across Europe. Queen Elizabeth I (1533–1603) had a distinctive look that encouraged nobles and peasants alike to emulate her embellished clothing, fair complexion and russet curls. Her gowns inspired other women to wear more exaggerated silhouettes of broad skirts, narrow bodices and high collars.

Marie Antoinette (1755–93) may be notorious for her excesses, but her style was hugely influential during her time at the French court. She was featured as the model for unauthorized fashion plates (an early form of fashion magazine). She popularized light muslin sashed dresses, which became known as a *chemise à la reine*. Her style was much emulated, which led her to commission increasingly extravagant gowns and cultivate more extreme looks (such as towering hairstyles) to stay ahead of trends. The fast pace of trends during Marie Antoinette's reign was a precursor to the rapid churn that the fashion industry faces today.

Other British monarchs created trends during their reigns: Queen Victoria popularized black for mourning, while Edward VIII's dapper style, as Prince of Wales, kick-started trends in Fair Isle knitwear; snap-brim hats; dinner jackets; the Windsor knot and collar; and, of course, the Prince of Wales check.

Despite the changing role of monarchy around the world, these elite figures can still be influential on trends. Britain's Duchess of Cambridge (formerly Kate Middleton) regularly wears British mid-range and designer brands – often demure dresses and simple, elegant footwear – boosting the popularity of certain items and causing them to sell out almost overnight, as was the case with a diamanté necklace from Zara in December 2013.

From top: Elizabeth I in full regalia, c.1575. Fashions begun at her court would be emulated by aristocrats and other wealthy subjects; The style of the Duchess of Cambridge is closely followed by media and fans. Items worn by her quickly sell out, like the inexpensive Zara necklace worn here.

Louis XIV in red-heeled shoes, which only the aristocracy were allowed to wear. Portrait by Hyacinthe Rigaud, 1701.

Sumptuary laws

In previous centuries, 'sumptuary' laws restricted the wearing of certain colours or materials to the nobility. These regulations affected how trends could spread to those lower down the social order.

* Elizabeth I created many sumptuary laws, such as restricting the wearing of ermine to royalty. Many of these were repealed by her successor, James I.

* Talons rouges (red-heeled shoes) were restricted to the upper classes by Louis XIV of France (1638–1715). He also dictated which materials members of his court could wear, and which silhouettes – the more restrictive the garments, the higher the rank.

* Only royalty or high-ranking nobles were allowed to wear gold cloth in many European nations, e.g. Britain, Russia, France, Austria, Prussia, Poland and Portugal.

* As part of his efforts to westernize Russia, Peter the Great (1672–1725) created 17 sumptuary laws that discouraged the wearing of Russian clothing at court or at home. Women at court were expected to adopt the German, Austrian and French fashions of the era.

Style tribes

'Style tribes' can influence the spread and perception of new fashion looks. Style tribes are groups of people united by a distinctive look, and are often seen as different from the mainstream. For this reason, they can be inspirational, scandalous and even laughable. Below are some key style tribes through the ages who have been as influential as they were outrageous.

Macaronis
Perhaps the first identified style tribe, Macaroni fops were outlandish dressers who came to attention in the mid-eighteenth century. Their heavily embellished and colourful clothing was adapted from foreign fashions seen on the 'Grand Tour' and was much mocked, but influential nonetheless.

Dandies
Dedicated followers of Beau Brummell's (1778–1840) precise and (relatively) pared-back style were known as dandies. Though this tribe arose in the late eighteenth and early nineteenth century, there is still a visible cadre of men taking great pride in the precise knotting of a tie or the cut of a jacket.

Beatniks
The Beat Generation were a group of artists, writers and thinkers during the late 1950s and early 1960s whose style was exemplified by simple, fitted pieces for both men and women, often in black. The style of beatniks in Paris inspired Yves Saint Laurent to create his ready-to-wear brand, Rive Gauche.

Hippies
Hippies began as a countercultural group rejecting the politics and consumerism of 1960s America, expressing their beliefs through brightly coloured, free-flowing, patterned and embellished clothing. Their aesthetic continues to inspire fashion designers and festival fashion.

Punks
Rebellious and iconoclastic, punk style was also hugely creative, repurposing materials such as rubber and leather, mixing up historical references and creating bold new hair and make-up styles. Decades after their heyday in the late 1970s and early 1980s, punks continue to inspire designer and street style.

Clockwise from top: Macaroni fops brought outlandish style back from their Grand Tours of Europe; The hippie look is defined by colourful prints, easy fabrics and pieces from across the globe. A wedding in New York, 1967; The dandies of Brazzaville, Congo, known as sapeurs; Studs, leather, spiky hair and a rebellious attitude define the punk style of the 1970s and 80s.

Celebrity influence

While we may live in a world of celebrity culture now, with every garment or accessory worn by famous people monitored and critiqued on social media and in the press, celebrities have long been style leaders. Today, as the influence of royalty has lost some of its sartorial power, celebrities have become one of our key reference points for trends.

Members of the elite were the first celebrities to influence fashion. Georgiana, Duchess of Devonshire (1757–1806), was known as the 'Empress of Fashion' in the late eighteenth century, popularizing trends for women wearing tall feathers in their hair and more relaxed belted muslin dresses. During the Regency period, Beau Brummell, a close friend of the ruling Prince of Wales, was much emulated for his pared-down and precise way of dressing, which turned the tide of over-the-top Georgian men's fashions.

Actors and actresses have long influenced fashion in their costumes and off-duty style, from Mrs Frances Abington in the Georgian period and Sarah Bernhardt during the Belle Epoque, to silver-screen sirens such as Clara Bow and Marlene Dietrich. Film star Joan Crawford's style was hugely influential in the 1920s and 30s: a dress she wore in the film *Letty Lynton* was copied by Macy's department store, and sold over 50,000 replicas. Since then, actors as diverse as Katharine Hepburn and Audrey Hepburn, Clark Gable, Brigitte Bardot, Steve McQueen, Pam Grier, Sarah Jessica Parker, James Dean, Chloë Sevigny and Sienna Miller have, in different ways, all influenced the way people dress.

Hollywood icons are not the only fashion influencers. India's Bollywood stars have long influenced fashions across south Asia and the Indian diaspora, from Madhubala wearing flowing *kurtas* and *churidars* in the 1960s to Kareena Kapoor in 2007 pairing a casual T-shirt with her *salwar* in *Jab We Met,* which influenced Indian street style for several years.

Musicians are another major influence on trends, from Josephine Baker's flapper style and Frank Sinatra's dapper looks to The Beatles' and Jimi Hendrix's colourful 1960s styles. In the 1970s, disco queens like Donna Summer led the way – followed by punk bands and New Romantics such as Adam Ant in the late 1970s and 1980s, and hip-hop pioneers Run-DMC, grunge icon Kurt Cobain, quirky Björk and 'queen of pop' Madonna in the 1990s and 2000s, together with youth influencers such as Britney Spears, Rihanna, Kanye West and many K-pop (Korean pop) bands such as 2NE1 and Big Bang.

Opposite, clockwise from top: Kanye West and Kim Kardashian at the 2015 MTV Video Music Awards, Los Angeles; Run-DMC's devotion to 'My Adidas' kick-started a trend for shell-toe sneakers; Joan Crawford's much-copied dress from the film Letty Lynton.

This page, from top: Two members of Korean band Big Bang at a Chanel catwalk show in Seoul, 2015; Beau Brummell's famously austere style, shown in this 1805 portrait, changed the way men dressed at the beginning of the Georgian era.

Celebrity stylist Rachel Zoe at work on an InStyle *shoot with actress Jaime King.*

Professional influence

It is now common for fashion designers, stylists and those who create costumes for characters in film and TV to have an impact on fashion, but for centuries these professions did not exist. Dressmakers and tailors would create useful, stylish or even influential garments for their clients, but these skilled creators would often be anonymous. In addition to fashion designers, other fashion professionals have been shaping the way people dress for many decades.

Rose Bertin, designer and stylist to Marie Antoinette, was perhaps the first famous professional to influence fashion at large. Bertin created looks for the queen that noble women then wanted her to emulate for them, meaning that Marie Antoinette would constantly commission something new and different to maintain her position as a style leader. Since then, fashion stylists (who help to put together looks for fashion brands and media) and celebrity stylists (who help the famous decide what to wear) have become more visible and influential in terms of trends.

Fashion stylists play an important role in influencing how fashion is worn, which can range from pairing a dress with trousers on the catwalk, to mixing designer pieces with activewear in fashion shoots. Fashion editors for magazines have long been influential in terms of choosing the key items for the season to be shown in their publications – with those working on high-profile titles such as *Vogue* or *Harper's Bazaar* having the widest influence, while those working on more cutting-edge magazines can help offer new visions for fashion that can influence consumers and other fashion professionals alike.

Celebrity stylists are the 'power behind the celebrity throne', choosing items for actors, musicians and other stars to help create looks that their fans will admire and emulate. Arianne Phillips has worked with Madonna for many years, creating iconic looks for her tours and videos for 'Frozen', 'Don't Tell Me' and 'Hollywood'. Marni Senofonte has worked to turn Beyoncé from a musical powerhouse into a fashion force too, helping to create the much-discussed looks for her 'visual albums'. Celebrity stylists are particularly important in creating stars' looks during awards season and for high-profile press events, with stylists such as Rachel Zoe and Nicola Formichetti gaining fashion fame as a result.

On screen, costume designers can influence trends. Early Hollywood costume designers such as Edith Head created many iconic looks for movies, which were widely emulated by consumers. Orry-Kelly put Humphrey Bogart in a white dinner jacket and a beat-up mackintosh in *Casablanca*, and dressed Marilyn Monroe in barely there frocks for *Some Like It Hot*. More recently, the costume choices made by Sandy Powell (*Carol, Cinderella*), Nolan Miller (*Dynasty*) Trish Summerville (*The Hunger Games* series), Colleen Atwood (*Memoirs of a Geisha, Chicago*), Patricia Field (*Sex and the City*), Janie Bryant (*Mad Men*) and Michele Clapton (*Game of Thrones*) have driven fashion trends across the globe.

Costumes from hit TV show Mad Men influenced fashion for men and women.

Social influences

Changing fashions and silhouettes act as an indicator of how we feel about ourselves and our world – ideas about status, wealth, philosophy, morality, religion, politics, art, science, nutrition, anatomy and sex can all affect trends. Three social factors – status, demographics and desirability – have more impact than any others.

Status

Throughout history, fashion has been as much about what clothes represent as about the garments themselves. In different cultures, certain materials or silhouettes can denote higher status or wealth (see 'Sumptuary laws', p.13) and, for many centuries, women's dress was used to display the wealth of their husbands. In modern fashion, designer clothing is often used as a marker of status, but there is frequently an aesthetic division between obvious status symbols, which can be seen as gaudy or nouveau riche, and more subtle symbols, such as ultra-fine cashmere or limited-edition sneakers, which denote status to those in the know.

Left to right: Portrait of Mrs Edmund Morton Playdell by Gainsborough, c.1765. For centuries, a family's wealth was displayed through the richness of women's dress; Today, status can be shown through visible symbols such as logos, or hidden ones, known as 'stealth wealth'.

Demographics

The ages, characteristics and beliefs of different groups within a society can influence trends. This is most clearly seen with youth culture. The rise of the teenager in the post-war period created new rock 'n' roll fashions and new style icons to emulate, fuelling an important and lucrative youth fashion market that continues to this day. The ideals and opinions of different generations can also influence trends. The millennial generation (those born between roughly 1980 and 2000), for example, who prize individuality, authenticity and creativity, have helped fuel many recent fashion trends, from niche brands and customization to 'athleisure' and gender-neutral dressing. Likewise, baby boomers (those born after World War II) have changed expectations of what older consumers want to wear, leading fashion retailers to create new stylish collections for the 60+ shopper.

Desirability

Left to right: The narrow-hipped, boyish style of the 1920s was seen as desirable and modern; The rise of the teenager after World War II created new styles, activities and aspirations.

Sex appeal has long been a driving factor for fashion trends. Different eras and cultures have different ideas of what makes someone look desirable, but their effect is often to accentuate a woman's breasts, waist or hips, or a man's shoulders or legs. There can also be trends in what body shapes are considered most attractive, which can affect how certain garments are constructed or worn. In previous centuries, for example, a rounded or well-padded figure was viewed as attractive as it showed the person was well fed, and therefore affluent. Since the 1920s, however, with the rise of the lithe and agile flapper style, slimness has been seen as more desirable, as it denotes discipline and delicacy. In recent years, a more toned physique has come into fashion as a way of showing a healthy lifestyle, giving rise to more body-conscious fashion.

The trends industry: past, present and future

Trend forecasting has existed for just over a century, beginning in the US and France. An industry that began by dictating trends has since changed its focus to inspiring trends, and responding to consumer needs.

The practice of tracking and forecasting trends began in 1915, when the first colour forecasts were created by American specialist Margaret Hayden Rorke. She would find out what colours were being produced by French textile mills (which dictated what was popular in Paris, and as a result in America), and create 'colour cards' to distribute to US manufacturers and retailers. Then, as now, the point of Hayden Rorke's colour forecasts was to help the fashion industry focus on what fashions were most likely to appeal to consumers, and thereby limit waste and markdowns. The first forecasts, however, by organizations such as the Textile Color Card Association of the United States and Tobe, told brands and retailers which colours to produce based on what other companies had created, and gave the consumer little choice. As such, trend reports effectively dictated what would be popular.

In the 1960s and 1970s, the purpose of trend forecasts shifted from narrowing choices for manufacturers (and therefore consumers) towards a more inspirational purpose. The forecasts became tactile: colourful and visionary books of ideas and design directions were produced, intended to inspire designers and manufacturers to create exciting new products – which produced both hits and misses. This era of forecasting gave rise to some of the industry's biggest names, such as Li Edelkoort (founder of Trend Union) and Nelly Rodi of the eponymous Paris-based agency, and to the idea of the 'trend guru'.

In 1998, a fashion-forecasting upstart changed the industry again. Worth Global Style Network (WGSN) was the first online trend service, and led the shift from physical, seasonal trend reports to fast-paced, international trend reporting and forecasting across multiple categories. In the same period, the industry's focus has shifted towards more consumer-led trends, wherein designers and retailers place more emphasis on the changing lifestyle of their consumer and aim to give them what they need, or will want. This means that lifestyle trends, or 'macro trend' research (which examines entertainment, culture, food, technology and design), have become a more important part of the trend process, alongside the colours and materials with which the first forecasters dealt.

Clockwise from top left: Slow Futures trend report cover from WGSN, 2018; Couture fashion plate with fabric swatches showing Schiaparelli designs, from Cahiers Bleu, Winter 1952, plate 17; From a trend book by PeclersParis, 1984.

23

From niche to mainstream skill

In the last hundred years, trend forecasting has evolved from a very niche set of specialist skills, purchased through a dedicated service, to a skill expected in many roles within the fashion business. The ability to spot and forecast trends is now required as part of the general design and production process, and is often augmented by the many online and physical trend services available.

Swatch cards from the
Color Association of the
United States, 1936.

Inspiration plus information

Recession and an increasingly global fashion market have made accurate forecasts more important than ever, leading many brands and retailers to blend their inspirational and forward-looking trend reports (whether in traditional book form or online) with 'smart' data ranging from in-house sales figures and social-media analysis to market reports.

This has led to services like Edited (for more, see profile on pp.106-7), and a greater expectation that trend forecasters can analyse the numbers of fashion trends as much as the style and mood. It is no longer enough for a trend forecast to be beautiful and inspiring – it must also be robust and applicable. According to Edited, this helps 'businesses plan for the future better and make decisions based on what the market is actually showing them'. But while data can show what has been successful, the nature of trends is about looking into the future – so those armed with both visionary forecasts and in-depth analytics will be best placed to offer inspiring product that will sell. 'Not information, but confirmation', as David Shah, founder of View Publications (see pp.134–35), puts it.

As such, there is now less reliance on one full-service trends agency, or a single trends guru. Instead, many brands and retailers conduct their own in-house research and forecasting, which is blended with trend forecasts by leading agencies and more specific directions from category specialists, such as denim forecaster Amy Leverton (see pp.44–45) or materials expert Barbara Kennington.

Timeline of the trends industry

1915
First colour cards created in the US

1927
Tobe Reports began

1963
Global colour panel Intercolor established with a head office in France

1967
French trend agency Promostyl launches its first trend book

1969
Doneger creates 'first trend forecast'

1998
First online trend service WGSN launches

2009
Edited launch

See also Agencies, companies and websites on pp.38–39.

2

The Trend Industry

In this chapter, we detail the key professional roles in the trend-forecasting industry and the variety of jobs within it, what their work involves and how they are all connected. We offer a summary of the current services, agencies, websites and experts, from global services to smaller niche companies.

Trend-forecasting agencies, websites and services aim to provide their clients with indispensable information to help them do their jobs efficiently and effectively. Some companies attempt to cover the whole of the fashion and design industries, from consumer research and macro trends looking forward 15 to 20 years through to on-the-season in-store retail analysis, while others focus on niche or single products, or just one discipline such as colour forecasting.

We also profile a select cross-section of industry insiders, and look in depth at their job roles and career paths in the trends industry and how they use trend forecasting in their daily lives.

We will also look at the difference between trend forecasting and trend reporting, as well as examining the types of report that a trend service may typically produce.

A round-table trend meeting at PeclersParis to determine the colour palettes for the season. Attendees are presenting their research and suggestions and collating their ideas as a whole.

Roles

This section details the key professional roles in the trend-forecasting industry, including colour, material and print experts to street-style specialists; retail, buying and merchandising experts; consumer analysts; and designers. We also explore the growing influence of non-professionals such as bloggers, vloggers and other online communities, and look at the impact of social media on trends in the fashion-design industry.

Colour forecasters

Colour forecasters form part of the core trend-forecasting industry. Through extensive research and analysis, they create palettes that inform the market, designers and ultimately the consumer which colours they feel will be important. A colour specialist creates a handful of palettes several seasons ahead, which influence multiple parts of the industry and kick-start the rest of the trend cycle.

Materials specialists

Materials specialists look at surfaces and the composition and texture of materials, woven or non-woven, and predict which surfaces will be most important over the coming seasons. Many materials specialists work with scientists and raw-product manufacturers, usually starting the process years in advance. They then work with colour forecasters at the start of the seasonal forecasts, producing a list of material influences that they can show to designers, manufacturers and suppliers to start off the sampling process.

Yarn and fibre specialists

Yarn and fibre specialists look at natural and man-made yarn, fibres and filaments before they are woven or knitted into actual textiles and materials to be made up into product samples. They use information from colour and materials specialists to decide what sort of material they should be creating, and add their own influences and inspirations.

Yarn and fibre specialists discuss new colours and threads at a trends event.

Print specialists

Print specialists look at printed surface decoration – be it digital, screenprinted, hand-drawn or transferred. From graphic pattern to complicated repeats and placement, print can take many forms. Print specialists use the information supplied by colour forecasters and materials specialists to inform their research, and they put together packs of inspirational material to guide print designers. Prints will then be created in-house, by freelancers or bought as samples at trade shows.

Surface specialists

Surface specialists look at all embellishment on textiles and materials, from embroidery to additional hardware such as sequins. They, too, work with information from colour and materials specialists, and then collaborate with suppliers and manufacturers. They work to get samples made to exhibit and sell at trade fairs and shows, where designers will pick them up to use in their collections.

Product designers

Product designers are trained specialists in their chosen field. They use colour, materials and macro trends to help inform their designs, drawing up shapes and silhouettes to be sampled and then made into garments or products. The list of product sectors is vast, but it can be roughly divided into womenswear, menswear, childrenswear, footwear, accessories, denim, intimates and swimwear, with each category often broken down by the designer into individual garment or product types.

A shoe designer draws up his initial ideas into sketch form after collating together all his initial research.

Patterns are cut and the logo is stamped onto a pocket detail of a bag in line with the agreed branding for the product in a pre-determined and carefully chosen colour.

Garment technologists and pattern cutters

Garment technologists ensure that each garment or item is technically correct, making sure that it fits and is fit for purpose. They also help in the design process, working with the pattern cutter to scale up patterns for production through pattern grading. Production managers then make sure that the designer's ideas and vision are manufactured in the best possible way.

Buyers

Buyers use their allocated budgets to purchase products for their shops in advance of each season, overseeing a delicate balance between what they hope to be bestsellers, core products and key special-purchase products. Buyers follow all current trends to make sure that the products they buy hit their optimum potential for the consumer while they are available in stores.

Merchandisers

Merchandisers decide when and where stock should be displayed within a store in order to achieve its best sales potential. They work closely with the buying team, so they know which stock and products will be arriving and when. They collaborate closely with the retail team to ensure their shop floors are working all the current trends and are at their most appealing to consumers. They also work with visual merchandisers – who dress the windows, mannequins and shop displays – and with graphic-design and marketing teams. They must keep abreast of trends in big-budget visual merchandising in larger stores globally, as well as with smaller niche retailers who are often more creative with their limited spaces and budgets.

Retailers

Retailers need an extensive knowledge of the market, from the high street to pop-up shops, as well as what will be opening up soon and how key destinations are changing. A retailer is likely to pull trends from sales data, catwalk or street reports as well as to travel globally in order to keep abreast of what competitors are doing. They also take inspiration from cutting-edge shops and popular retail destinations to help them decide what to prioritize in store, as well as how the shop should look. Retailers also need to keep abreast of consumer analytics as well as sales data, to make sure they are targeting the right consumers with the right products in the right way.

Key roles within fashion trend forecasting

Industry role

Colour specialist	Materials, yarn and fabric specialists	Print and surface specialists	Product designers	Garment technologists, pattern cutters and production managers	Buyers and merchandisers	Retail consumers and youth specialists	Marketing and press

Trend services used by each role

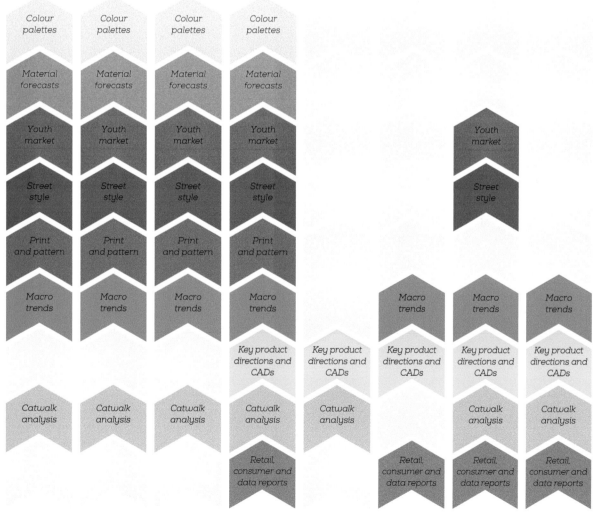

Marketers

Marketers turn consumers into customers, and are responsible for marketing products on behalf of a brand or business. They work with the product-design teams, buyers and merchandisers to understand the trends they are working with, what the key 'stories' are and how they can best portray these to the customer through graphic design, displays and promotional materials. Marketing has more to do with creating a demand for a product than with actually getting customers to buy, but it does, of course, have a direct influence on the latter activity. Marketers must keep themselves in line with the trends in graphic styles and key market influences as well as socio-economic trends that can affect consumers' spending patterns.

Consumer analysts

Consumer analysts continuously watch the market and how it flows, analysing buying trends alongside variable factors such as socio-economics, the political climate, and art and design trends. They identify market segmentation through similarities of consumers' needs, wants and demands based on demographics, spending behaviour and geographic differences. Consumer analysts will study data from across the retail world and publish reports, commentary and tailored information for macro trends within the business or for strategic planning by brands.

Youth specialists

Youth specialists focus on emerging trends seen on the streets through street-style photography; youth-market inspirations like festivals, emerging musicians and fashion labels; and television, films and online channels from which the younger market may take inspiration. Youth specialists often work with brands to help identify what the youth market is interested in, and what the current generation may be likely to purchase in the years to come as their disposable income grows.

Graphic designers

Graphic designers create season, collection or campaign imagery, illustration and text design that can be used by marketers, retailers and merchandisers to aid them in the selling process.

The blogger Susie Bubble is often photographed in the street and hailed for her sense of style and taste as well as her ability to discover new and upcoming brands.

Social media

Bloggers

Bloggers run informational or personal-opinion sites. They have become increasingly influential within fashion, with brands often working with key bloggers to launch products – trusting their opinions and those of their followers over the word of professionals. Star bloggers may launch their own product ranges or work in collaboration with major brands. Examples include Parisian Garance Doré, who collaborated with US brand Kate Spade; US blogger Leandra Medine from Man Repeller, who launched a range with Dannijo; and the UK's Susie Bubble from Style Bubble, working with the Swedish brand Monki. Others have become stars through the power of their blogs. Tavi Gevinson became famous for her Style Rookie blog at the age of 12 and is now an actor; Marc Jacobs named a handbag after Philippines-based Bryanboy's blog. Trend agencies use blogs to gather cutting-edge information about particular subjects or new product releases, or to keep abreast of a specific demographic's opinions and interests.

Vloggers

Vlogs are used in a similar way to blogs; vloggers use video to populate their sites with commentary, information or 'how-to' tutorials. A huge variety of channels is available, the most popular being devoted to beauty. Vlogging stars count their followers in the millions, and, like bloggers, have entered the world of brand endorsement, collaboration and offline fame. Tanya Burr, best known for her beauty channel on YouTube, has launched her own cosmetics line as well as publishing a book on beauty.

Tumblr

Tumblr feeds allow users to add a rolling selection of imagery with limited or no word content. They are a good way to get an author's personal style across with ease. They can also be used to showcase niche interests, or can contain humorous feeds. Trend forecasters use Tumblr feeds to help inspire the design process.

Pinterest

Pinterest showcases images taken from or uploaded to the Internet, and lets people curate boards of interest. Made popular by the fashion, food and wedding industries, Pinterest is now regularly used by brands and retailers to market their products and to sell directly to customers – either through their own boards or by asking or paying for key users to Pin their products. Star Pinners have hundreds of boards and millions of followers, so their brand worth is crucial.

Instagram

An image-based social-media platform, Instagram was made popular by people who post inspirational images as well as selfies, images of themselves. It is now one of the most important channels through which brands can showcase their products when worn by stars with huge followings. Many fashion brands use Instagram stars to promote their products on their image feeds. Stars such as Gigi Hadid have accelerated their modelling careers through the channel. Instagram is most useful for trend agencies, who use it for visual inspiration and also for its network, linking individuals and products; users can link through into unknown or untapped information, and view launches as soon as they appear.

Snapchat

Snapchat is a photo and video service that allows users to add a caption and send to friends, with the content disappearing after 24 hours. It is most popular with the millennial market (those aged 18–34), and the 2016 US presidential campaign featured heavily on the service. It has a magazine-style section of curated content, with which brands are becoming heavily involved.

From top: Pinterest boards are an excellent tool for organizing research and initial trend ideas in one place; An example of an Instagram page from the footwear and accessories trend service Quartermastertrends.

The influence of social media

Brands were quick to use the enormous rise in the popularity of social media to raise their profiles, increase their supporters and ultimately revenue streams. They also try to affiliate themselves with the most popular members or with those they think are their brands' best fit. The variety of ways in which brands can use the various channels is vast, with the most basic being simple advertising, pop-up ads, cookie-influenced banners and consumer-targeted content.

Many brands have teamed up with prolific star bloggers and vloggers who have become famous purely through their online channels – whether they are commenting on style, design or beauty, or are reviewing product. Many use the following tactics to help engage their customers:

* Competition-style giveaways;

* User-generated content or celebrity/ star takeovers, when a celebrity curates or edits part of a brand's website;

* Collaborations and endorsements;

* Online parties and events such as Pin or Twitter parties;

* Becoming brand or channel ambassadors.

Model agencies may add social-media clauses to contracts to ensure that their clients' campaigns are further promoted by their models, thereby utilizing the power of models' personal networks for their clients. Many individual users with no previous link to products or planned online presence have found themselves instant Internet stars. Pinterest, for example, picked a selection of Pinners whose boards they liked and promoted them on their pages. Some relatively unknown users gained millions of followers almost overnight, some of whom, such as Maryann Rizzo and Danaë Vokolos, have gone on to change their careers or be approached by brands to place Pins on their behalf.

Social media has also spawned an entire market for branding and consultancy agencies, which tailor brands' social-media content and strategy as well as linking them to suitable celebrities or online personalities. There are also sites devoted to linking brands to pay-per-click revenue streams for many platforms – mainly blogs – that allow the latter's publishers to take a percentage of any sales gained; such is the case with the site Bloglovin'. Pinterest added their 'buyable Pins' buttons on select e-commerce platforms in 2015, opening up the market to smaller e-tailers wishing to sell to customers direct outside brands' own sites. This development could even negate the wholesale process as we currently know it.

Reporting vs. forecasting

Trend reporting and forecasting can be confused. Trend reporting is the 'say what you see' approach to what is in the market at that moment, whereas trend forecasting examines how the market will look in a few months or years. Like forecasting, reporting usually includes some analysis, for example the spotting of similar styles or colours on a catwalk, but its influence is limited to the current season.

Trend reporting is an important tool used by many agencies and in many roles. It is a useful way of tracking how retailers and consumers are responding to key trends – which are being featured most in magazines or shop windows, and how well they are selling. There are four key trend-reporting methods.

Comp shopping
Retailers will often compare how key trends are being used by their competitors; this is called comp shopping. They may compare how a certain colourway or take on a trend is selling or being promoted in competitors' stores, and adjust their own design and buy accordingly. Designers and buyers may also look at competitors' stores to see if any product is lacking in their own ranges.

Shop windows
Trend services and in-house teams go to key cities and neighbourhoods to photograph which brands, colours, styles and trends are being featured in the windows of influential retailers, including department stores, boutiques and major retailers. These images help them assess how well a certain trend is being received by the market, because the pieces that retailers choose to promote in their windows can have a considerable effect on consumer desire.

Sales data
Buyers and merchandisers (and sometimes design teams) track how well key items, colours and shapes are selling, which may influence whether they create new versions of a product to take advantage of consumer interest, through new colourways, fabrications, silhouettes, etc. Likewise, data can help brands and retailers decide if a product is worth repeating next season.

Consumer media
Consumer media – such as fashion magazines, blogs and websites – focus on products that are currently, or soon to be, available to shoppers, and can therefore offer a useful view on which trends are likely to be important within a season. However, they are unable to predict their longevity.

Trend reports

Trend services provide a range of different reports. The typical types of report are listed below, starting from the early inspiration stage. Each trend service may give their report a different name.

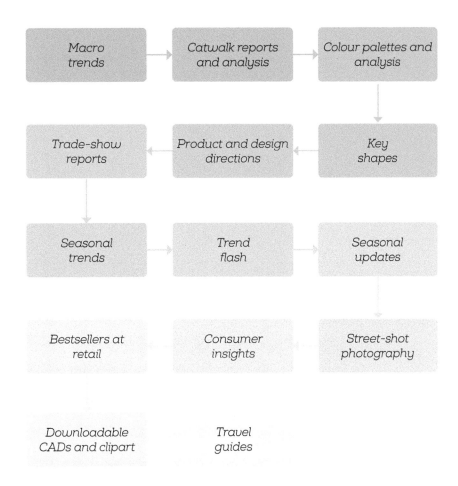

Agencies, companies and websites

There are thousands of trend services, agencies, websites and experts. This list, from leading services like WGSN, Peclers and Promostyl to key influencers such as Li Edelkoort and specialist trend forecasters such as Anna Starmer and smaller niche services, are useful or interesting.

Anna Starmer (UK)
Anna Starmer is predominantly a colour forecaster who also runs a creative consultancy working on design trends, bespoke reports and in-house design direction.
www.annastarmer.com

Faith Popcorn's Brain Reserve (US)
Brain Reserve is a future-insight and marketing consultancy started in 1974 by Faith Popcorn, who is recognized as one of the United States' foremost trend experts. Brain Reserve works with clients to help them create the products of tomorrow, and offers a Trendbank service that aims to help predict the behaviours of future consumers.
www.faithpopcorn.com

Five by Fifty (Singapore)
Five by Fifty is based in Singapore, and focuses on the Asia Pacific region (APAC). It operates Asian Consumer Intelligence, a trend analysis site dedicated to the Asia Pacific.
www.fivebyfifty.com

The Future Laboratory (UK)
The Future Laboratory styles itself as a consultancy that helps organizations to future-proof by harnessing market trends and responding to consumers' needs to stay ahead of the market. Its subscription-based service, LS:N Global, conducts biannual consumer briefings, as well as daily updated observation and trend reporting.
www.thefuturelaboratory.com

Iconoculture (US)
A US-based, global consumer-insight specialist, with an emphasis on data and demographics.
www.iconoculture.com

Nelly Rodi (France)
Nelly Rodi is a trend-forecasting agency that uses consumer, creative and market intelligence to produce forecast reports for clients, as well as to update its NellyRodiLab website with daily insights.
www.nellyrodi.com

PeclersParis (France)
PeclersParis is a Parisian innovation, style and consulting agency started in 1970. It is one of the only agencies still to produce trend books – as all agencies did pre-Internet – and also offers a consulting arm with trend analysis, brand strategy and style consulting.
www.peclersparis.com

Pej Gruppen (Denmark)
Pej Gruppen is a Scandinavian trend institute, founded in 1975, whose members claim to 'spot, analyse and communicate future trends to professionals in the lifestyle industries'. It publishes a selection of trend and insight magazines for the design industries as well as holding seminars and talks, creating reports and working on a wide range of consultancy projects.
www.pejgruppen.com

Promostyl (France)
Established in 1966 in Paris, Promostyl claims to be the original trend agency and the first to launch trend books. It now has numerous global offices, including several in China. It started as a service to fabric and trim manufacturers wanting to gain opportunities in the ready-to-wear market, and now offers a consultancy and brand-development service.
www.promostyl.com

Quartermaster (US/UK)

A trend forecasting agency supplying pertinent trends for the global footwear and accessories industries. They provide insight reports and colour, material and trend analysis, as well as range building and product development for brands and retailers.
www.quartermastertrends.com

Scout (Australia)

Based in Sydney, Scout is a boutique agency that 'combine[s] global market insight with creativity to bring ... results-based, proven forecasts' for the fashion and design industries. With a focus on the retail industries, Scout has a personal and interactive approach to its work.
www.scout.com.au

Stylus (UK)

Stylus is an innovation research and advisory firm that runs a subscription-based website with content covering all aspects of fashion and product design, as well as an advisory service for tailored information and innovation forums.
www.stylus.com

Trendbüro (Germany)

Trendbüro is a strategic think tank that uses social, economic and consumer trends to create effective marketing strategies for its clients. Trendbüro is part of the global communications agency Avantgarde.
www.trendbuero.com

Trendstop (UK)

Trendstop combines an online trend-research platform with a consultancy service and design studio whose 'expertise is in translating trend concepts into commercially successful products'.
www.trendstop.com

Trend Union (The Netherlands)

Trend Union is the trend studio of Dutch curator, trend innovator and leading light, Lidewij Edelkoort. Edelkoort has been a seminal figure in the trends world, and is well renowned for her live presentations and well-loved publications. Trend Tablet is Trend Union's social-media platform, which explains the trends process and hosts a community of designers, trend hunters and innovators.
www.trendtablet.com

Unique Style Platform (UK)

USP 'offers intelligent analysis to the fashion and style industries'. It has a free, daily blog service that engages clients, who then pay for a premium service offering seasonal trend forecasts and insight reports.
www.uniquestyleplatform.com

WGSN (US/UK)

Worth Global Style Network (WGSN) is one of the original online trend services, running since 1998. It bought out its main rival, Stylesight, in 2014, to become the largest service in the industry. The agency includes services such as WGSN Instock, which tracks stock and selling patterns and behaviour globally in real time across a wide range of retailers, while WGSN Style Trial allows buyers to test out their ranges on a live audience ahead of launch to retail.
www.wgsn.com

Industry profile
Tessa Mansfield

Biography
Tessa Mansfield is Content and Creative Director of global fashion and lifestyle trend service Stylus.

How did you end up in your current role?
I studied 3D design at Brighton University, specializing in plastics, materials and visual research, before manufacturing my own range of plastic products and working on the launch of *Wallpaper** magazine. This led to employment at Seymour Powell and SPForesight (SPF) from the late 1990s, working on an early form of visual trend research. I joined Stylus in 2010 as one of the founding team. Today, I head the content team, directing our content and creative strategy. We identify and connect the most important global and cross-industry trends for around 500 clients, including Reebok, Adidas, Marriott, Volvo, Moët Hennessy, Sephora and John Lewis.

How do you approach trend research and the forecasting process?
I see trends as simplifications of more complex realities, created by identifying patterns and themes. Trends provide businesses with compelling narratives, visual inspiration and social context from which they can create product, and against which they can measure their brand.

We do a variety of types of trend analysis at Stylus, for different audiences. Demographic or psychographic trends can provide context for a business when considering its future audience and what motivates them. Aesthetically driven trends can provide strong direction for all types of creative professional, from buyers to visual merchandisers.

The range of our trend reporting is wide, from blog posts to longer-term cross-industry consumer macro trends. To meet the timelines for manufacture and supply in design, we create Design Directions, Colour and Material Trends and Fashion Forecasts that look up to 18 months ahead. These visual reports are an inspirational product development tool, looking at everything from colour, finish and material through to graphic and spatial design.

What tools and resources do you and your teams use most in your research?
Our expert analysts observe influencers, read prolifically, speak to thought leaders and industry experts, collate information from across the Internet, find case studies to illustrate ideas, and incorporate stats from external quantitative research. The tools of desk research are an ever-growing set of web feeds, from blogs and social media to news.

We digest information as a team, to open up discussion and debate, hosting trend days and industry round tables where we invite external experts, opinion leaders and influencers to present, share and analyse trends alongside our in-house team. The team attend 150+ global cross-industry events per year – a mix of trade shows, design weeks, seminars and conferences. Over time, this allows us to see the evolution of products and ideas, which provides a strong source of trend knowledge.

How are Stylus trends translated into practical insights for clients?
There's so much trend information in the public realm that our role in offering curated analysis is critical to helping our clients cut through the noise. We give them the information they need to design new products and judge internal innovation. The visual element is so important. We present our design directions through beautiful proprietary mood boards, and we use infographics (see opposite) to bring less visual research to life. Demonstrating the rigour behind our analysis is important. Our reports contain future insights that plot the trajectory of a trend and its impact on particular industries.

How do you think the usage of trends is changing for the fashion industry?

Today, there's more emphasis on substantiating trend forecasts. While our reporting is largely qualitative, we support it through quantitative research and expert validation. Reporting from the catwalk is still a crucial part of our fashion delivery. Our clients like catwalk analysis as it confirms our forecast and is fast-response. But catwalks will become less relevant now that everyone can access them.

The fashion industry has become quite practical, appreciating that you can't look at fashion in isolation. By defining the key external influences that are shaping fashion today, linking to wider social and cultural trends, we help our clients build new business strategies. Forecasting will remain a critical commercial tool in understanding change in an increasingly volatile and fragmenting world.

How do fashion trends intersect with those from other categories?

There are complementary sectors – those you look at closely for direct correlation – versus those further afield that can provide broader inspiration and a more disruptive influence. In fashion forecasting, the complementary sectors have tended to be beauty, colour and materials, and interior design. Now we see more influence from technology, media and transportation, to name a few.

Industry profile
Ingrid De Vlieger

Biography

After studying business communication and working in various marketing-oriented roles, Ingrid started working for JanSport in product marketing ten years ago. She loved the product development element and moved to Eastpak in Belgium as a product assistant. Eight years later she is still at Eastpak, as Design and Development Manager.

How do you approach seasonal research and the trend process?

Identifying trends is a continuous process and requires constant observations. Looking for trends requires curiosity and interest in a wide array of subjects and this is why we also go through different channels to define our seasonal trends, and continue this throughout the year.

Do you have a methodology?

Defining the theme of a collection comes from hunting and collecting information the whole year round, but we also do a lot of seasonal activities from attending fairs to consulting trend books and working with trend agencies on a specific season. So our preparations towards a full collection is a mix of seasonal-specific research and what we catch over the full year. I'm constantly triggered by images and I have a small stock collected over the years that I keep and use for development. Next to this I think personal intuition is key – to look at the trend, follow your feeling and put yourself in the shoes of the Eastpak consumer.

To prepare the seasons we work with different trend agencies who are in different locations from Paris, London and Zurich to Japan and Korea. We consult trend books that describe the trends in colours, fabrics, shapes and styles and we work with digital fashion platforms to discover future consumer trends. We visit fairs – from fashion-related, to product design/innovation, interior and so on – as we feel it's important to have a wide scope of subjects. We complete regular market visits as the concept of discovering trends is also location specific: style differs from city to city. We go from Scandinavia to Paris, to London and Milan but also cities like Hong Kong, Seoul and Tokyo. We also do continuous online desk research, which quickly and inexpensively allows us to dig out data and inspiration from a wide variety of sources. Sometimes a single image can be so powerful that it triggers you and leads you to a full new collection! We work with our vendors and fabric suppliers, who keep us updated on new techniques and fabrics.

Which sectors of the industry do you find most inspiring for your work, be they social, cultural or aesthetic?

Looking for trends requires looking into a wide range of subjects but we are mostly inspired by the fashion scene, interior design, shoes or accessories.

How do you think the usage of trends is changing for the fashion industry?

Today, trends are born and die really fast. On social media consumers talk a lot about what is in and what is out. That is why it is really important we keep on consulting expert trend forecasters in this matter. They are already telling us we need to slow down on this. Nowadays the fashion and lifestyle industries also acknowledge the importance of good solid design and icons that don't disappear or fade. Hence we need to be bold and daring when we want to go for a more progressive collection.

What inspires you most?

I think for me travelling around and going into the field is a huge inspiration! Taking ideas from many different cities around the world and sharing the inspiration with the full team. It is great to see how different cultures translate different trends and colours. London will always differ from Tokyo and even the northern part of Europe is so different from the south.

It's very interesting. It's fun to put together all these pieces of the puzzle and come up with great collections.

What tools – website, blog, book, place, object – can you not be without?
WGSN, Highsnobiety, Hypebeast, trend books, fairs, cities around the world ... a mix of everything is the best platform to find inspiration on styles, colours and trends.

Please describe your current role and explain how trends play a part in that both literally and subconsciously.
In my current job I am responsible for designing and developing Eastpak product lines and collections. I need to meet the needs of the target consumers but also market requirements in terms of price, distribution and brand positioning. Together with the product team I manage the entire product design and development process from design input to samples. In this process market knowledge and trend research is the base. It is where the full process starts from.

Industry profile
Amy Leverton

Biography
Amy Leverton is an LA-based denim expert who specializes in consulting for denim brands. She has worked in the industry for ten years, most recently at WGSN as Director of Denim and Youth Culture.

What do you do now?
I am a trend consultant, brand strategist, journalist, copywriter and author, all for the denim industry.

How did you end up in trend forecasting?
I studied as a fashion designer and spent four years designing casualwear and denim, but my strength was always with research: mood boards, trend, initial concept and ideas, all the things that come before the design. In 2008 I interviewed at WGSN for Associate Denim Editor and luckily got the job.

What do your clients need from a trend forecast?
Recently the goalposts have changed quite dramatically. It used to be that they needed to know the emerging trends in enough time to react: silhouette, wash, colour, styling, etc. We're now going through a period of huge fluctuations and diversity of trend. Of course there are still emerging trends, such as the cropped flare, which brands can react to, but more and more I am finding that the sheer diversity of trends is confusing brands. Now they need more tailored information and help with strengthening their brand DNA, to know what trends to put their money behind and what to leave.

How does that change how you research things?
Since going freelance I read a lot more! In a constantly shifting industry, it's important to be aware of how things are changing, not just in trend but in business. I write a monthly article for Heddels denim blog where I explore industry shifts in retail, education, trade, fabric innovations and so on. This interaction with consumers and also with industry experts during the research process has really helped to enrich my global knowledge.

Do you always have denim in mind when you're researching or do you start off with more of a general view?
I start with a general, cultural view but of course I am always entrenched in denim so often it all goes hand in hand.

How do you approach trend research and the forecasting process?
Live it. That's it really. If you enjoy what you do, you never stop thinking, never stop looking, never stop being curious. I feel that as long as I still love what I do, to live is to research. Life is one big research project!

Do you have a methodology?
I subscribe to a few good newsletters such as BoF (businessoffashion.com), PSFK (psfk.com), etc. I Pin like crazy and I follow Instagram feeds that I feel keep me in the loop. I also think that a great network of industry friends goes a very long way. The more contacts you have, the more connected you are with every level of the market. People send me stuff, tag me in pictures and include me in conversations.

Which sectors of the industry do you find most inspiring for your work, be they social, cultural or aesthetic?
Right now I want to build my knowledge of the global supply chain, so mills, laundries, manufacturers and so forth. I am increasingly interested in transparency as far as production and manufacturing are concerned and industrial waste in the denim industry. I think this will be important in the future.

What trend forecasting services do you use, either professionally or personally?
I don't use trend forecasting services as I am one! I look at everything outside of the subscription-only format but every so often, if I am working on something specific I might have a little poke around on a site as confirmation. But more as a voyeur than anything.

How do you think the usage of trends is changing for the fashion industry?
I think there is definitely a huge return to brand transparency, authenticity and strong brand DNA. Gen Z are a suspicious lot and are often anti-corporation, anti-austerity and politically minded. They've grown up in a world of free information, so their needs are totally different to those of previous generations.

What inspires you most?
New talent I guess. Nothing gets my blood pumping faster than discovering a new brand doing something great in denim. I am also a massive fabric and weave geek and fabric innovation is so exciting right now.

What tools – website, blog, book, place, object – can you not be without?
Instagram and Pinterest.

EXERCISE: ANALYSE A CURRENT TREND

This exercise will help you to see that there is no right or wrong way to publish a trend report and that different trend services, blogs or individuals may report on the same trend in very different ways. Take a current and well-published trend, look at how a trend service has reported it and write a short report of no more than 500 words, backing up your findings with a selection of images from a variety of sources. Try and pick something that is inspiring street style, the high street or high-end fashion brands.

Be critical in your response to the method of reporting, and explain why you chose it. Is it, in your opinion, useful or inspiring? Is it an analysis, a review or a comment on a current trend? Who has the agency staff written it for? What is their target audience, and what do they want their readers to get out of the report?

Does your example give a clue as to where the idea came from? And where it is going? Would you have done it any better, or differently?

Take note of the following in your exercise:

∗ Images   *∗ Length*

∗ Wording   *∗ Title*

∗ Layout

Opposite: Colour palettes and material direction forecasts from trend service Scout.

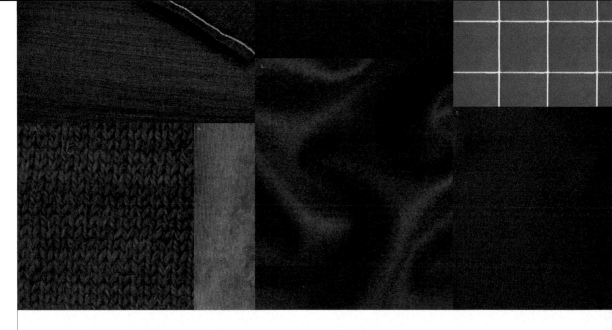

COLOUR palette

CORE: indigo + rich

A rich, deep autumnal palette with nautical inspired navy blues, the key colour statement. The dark navy replaces black, plus classic French navy, use accordingly. The deep plum is a new shade for smart tailoring and knitwear. The ginger adds punch to the group and works in wovens and knits in solids or colour blocked combinations with the other shades.

ACCENTS: lively + fresh

The accents add another level of colour into the mix with white a key accent for crisp shirting and fresh tees, plus nautical stripes. Use in solids for fashion pieces, including pants. The orange is a new highlight for tops, while the lighter teal is important for better-end products and fabrics in uniform inspired tailoring. The greyed-off blue is an alternative to navy and for more casual styling.

BOXED
COLOUR CARD

CORE:
Indigo + rich

PANTONE® 19-3922 TCX
Sky Captain

PANTONE® 17-1052 TCX
Roasted Pecan

PANTONE® 19-3815 TCX
Evening Blue

PANTONE® 19-2420 TCX
Pickled Beet

ACCENTS:
Lively + fresh

PANTONE® 11-0601 TCX
Bright White

PANTONE® 16-1349 TCX
Coral Rose

PANTONE® 18-4417 TCX
Tapestry

PANTONE® 19-4014 TCX
Ombre Blue

3

Trend Basics

Fashion may be the industry most associated with trends because of the highly visible way that ideas and designs evolve in seasonal catwalk shows, advertising campaigns and in-store collections, but trends are increasingly influential in other industries too. This book focuses on fashion trends, but Chapter 5 will explore how fashion and lifestyle trends influence each other.

The lessons learned from fashion-trend forecasting can be applied to other lifestyle categories such as travel, automotive products, food and beverages, and home and technology. The success of each of these industries lies in understanding evolving consumer desires, influences and aesthetics – in short, the zeitgeist. Zeitgeist, a German word meaning 'the spirit of the age', is one of the most important things for any trend forecaster to understand and exploit. An appreciation of zeitgeist forms the basis of trend forecasting: tapping into the subtle shifts in the way people behave or dress enables us to map where ideas will come from and project what their impact might be. In a practical sense, trend forecasting is gleaning what will inspire designers and other key influencers, and how these inspirations are turned into product that appears in stores and in consumers' wardrobes.

In this chapter, we look at how trends develop and the flow of information that influences them; we will give an overview of the key trend influencers, and explore how trends can evolve at different paces to become classics, seasonal trends or mere fads.

Catwalk shows are still highly influential, and many fashion professionals attend student shows to see new ideas. Yasemin Cakli final collection, University of Westminster 2016.

How trends spread

What is a trend?

Trend (noun)
A pattern or direction of change: a way of behaving or dressing that is developing or becoming more visible.

Something that is popular or fashionable at a given time. This could be the popularity of a certain 'key' item, way of dressing (styling) or colour combination.

No matter whether we are idly people-watching or consciously acting as cultural sponges, we absorb what other people around us are doing and wearing. When one person takes inspiration from another, incorporating part of that person's look into their own, they are going one step further and fostering a trend, whether consciously or otherwise.

Several writers have theorized why and how trends spread, and their models can help us to understand the progression of a trend – from one person trying out a new way to dress, to a group of people adopting it as a new style, to the idea hitting the catwalk, the shopfloor and then the masses on the streets (followed by the sale rail). This rise and fall of a trend is also known as the product life cycle.

Everett Rogers' diffusion-of-innovation theory suggests that ideas such as trends start with a small group of 'innovators', who then spread the idea to 'early adopters'. The latter form the gateway to the 'early majority', who bring a trend to its peak before it is taken on by the 'late majority', and eventually the few 'laggards' who have not yet tried it. The trend then fades, often to be replaced by a new one.

Rogers' diffusion-of-innovation theory

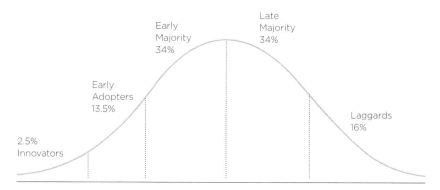

A successful trend will spread from early adopters to the mass market and late adopters, either naturally or through the encouragement of trend forecasters and brands. Not all trends are successful, however, and may be limited in their influence because they are too niche; too expensive; too controversial; or, conversely, too dull.

Good trend forecasters will spot the beginnings of a trend at the innovator or early-adopter stage, which should allow enough leeway to analyse and develop it into product form in time for mass-market interest.

The trend-forecasting schedule

Trend forecasters tend to operate at the beginning of the creative process, with their research informing and inspiring the designers, buyers and producers who will actually create the product. This forecasting work may be conducted by trend agencies, who create and supply colour, material, print and macro-trend reports (among others), or by in-house design teams as part of their research process.

Trend forecasters work 18–24 months ahead of the season for most fashion collections. For example, for a collection due to hit stores for spring/summer 2018, trend forecasters start research and analysis as early as summer 2016.

This schedule gives enough time for mills – the first step in the production process – to produce the necessary coloured and textured yarns and materials that shape trend development. Performance and sportswear, outerwear and fabric producers often have longer lead times than 18–24 months. Such products tend to be more technical in nature than others, using a more time-intensive process and possibly involving new technologies or surface treatments, which may take longer to develop and test than something straightforward like a cotton jersey T-shirt.

Once forecasters have reviewed mill colours and available materials at trade events such as Première Vision, and have identified key directions, they then forecast the print, pattern and key shapes which are turned into design samples. Then, working with buyers and merchandisers, designers develop their ideas into a full product collection, from which retailers choose items to place in store and marketers select which pieces to promote through advertising and public relations (PR).

Trends are examined at different points in the production process, with each stage feeding the next. Insights from agency or in-house specialists help to develop and realize trends at different stages, as detailed below.

Trends timeline

Yarn/fibre	Macro trends	Print	Range development
Materials, fabric and knitwear manufacturers	A cross-section of industry specialists (colour, materials, consumer/lifestyle researchers, designers)	(18-12 months ahead) Graphics and print designers	Product designers, buyers and merchandisers, technical production specialists

24 months ahead	20 months ahead	18 months ahead	12 months ahead	6 months ahead

Colour/materials		Product design	Shop floor
Colour, material and surface forecasters		Clothing, accessories, lifestyle and home designers	Sales staff, PR, marketing, visual merchandisers

Changing timelines

While 18–24 months is the standard period of time between the inception and realization of a trend – to allow sufficient time for all of the elements shown on p.51 to transpire – trend timelines are now speeding up.

Real-time catwalks
Catwalk coverage was once closed to all but fashion professionals. The wealth of coverage now available online and through social media means that consumers see new trends as soon as they hit the runway, without waiting 3–6 months for editors and stylists to filter the millions of outfits into digestible trends for shoppers. As a result, consumers' appetite for the latest trends is accelerating – they are increasingly unwilling to wait months for new designer collections to arrive in store, while the millions of people who buy the 'fast-fashion' versions of key trends expect them to be delivered just as rapidly.

Rapid retail
While many designer brands are still working to the idea that autumn/winter collections shown on catwalks in February and March will hit stores in August, fast-fashion brands such as Zara can get trends from catwalk to global stores in just a few weeks, thanks to smart production models. This means that trends can get out of sync, as consumers demand the newest ideas from the runway regardless of what season they come from – a colour from the autumn/winter collection may end up in stores a few short months after it has been shown on catwalks, instead of the traditional six-month wait.

In a bid to prevent customer ennui, brands such as Burberry and House of Holland allow customers to order the looks they like straight off the catwalk, while luxury e-tailer Net-a-Porter and online trunk show Moda Operandi allow people to pre-order key looks, which are sent direct to shoppers a few weeks or months later – often before they hit stores.

Trend tracking
To counteract the effect of getting left behind consumers' ideas, many retailers now use close-to-season or in-season trend tracking that offers real-time reports on key colours, silhouettes and products. This allows brands and retailers to create products to fit that trend before it runs out of steam.

Types of trend

Trends can last a short or long time, and are usually separated into fads, trends and classics. The graph below illustrates the different paces of trend development.

Fads tend to spring up quickly and fade rapidly, going from early adoption to mass market in a few short weeks or months, while trends grow more slowly – often over the course of several seasons or even years. This is the 'sweet spot' for trend forecasters, as a trend evolving over the course of 1–2 years gives enough time for it to be turned into marketable product (see 'Trends timeline', p.51).

A trend can succeed because it is new and interesting, but it only gains longevity if it offers deeper meaning and usefulness to people's lives. The recent vogue for wearing highly technical trainers with any outfit, for example, keys into a continuing consumer desire for function and ease.

Opposite: Burberry Prorsum catwalk show, Spring/Summer 2016, at which Burberry introduced catwalk-to-consumer direct sales for the first time.

The development of fads, trends and classics

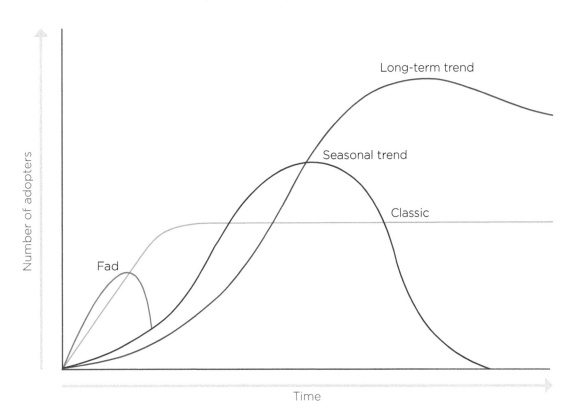

Fads: 3–6 months

A fad is a niche look or product with a short lifespan (often only a few months). Faddish items are often regarded as 'must-have' at the time, but consumers tire of them quickly and are unlikely to make repeat purchases: a single item is normally enough to satisfy consumers' need to feel fashionable.

In many cases, the faster a trend blows up, the faster it burns out. Fads often have a quirky or novelty product at their core that has limited usefulness (or wearability, in fashion terms). Another factor that restricts fads from becoming trends, or even classics, is that they have limited audience appeal; they are only interesting or accessible to a certain group of people, such as urban teenagers or fashion insiders. Key fashion fads include the 1980s puffball skirt, the Nu Rave look of the late 2000s or the super-plain Normcore look of 2014.

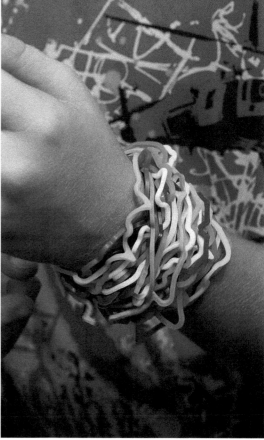

Trends: 6 months–5 years

A trend is a style or category of products that becomes popular for a period of time, and influences a wide range of consumers, brands and even product types. Key trends will be adopted by many people before losing popularity and becoming obsolete – or worse, uncool.

The life cycle of a fashion trend can vary, but successful examples last at least one season (seasonal trends) or continue to develop into new forms or become adopted by new consumer groups for several years (long-term trends), as was the case with high-platform heels or performance wear. Unlike a fad, a trend has the potential to have long-term influence, or even to become a new classic.

Seasonal trends: 6–12 months

These are often catwalk-inspired trends that manifest as key items, colours, silhouettes or ways of styling an outfit. They become the dominating looks during the season – such as wearing double denim or a 'couture sweatshirt' – but they drift out of favour after 6 to 12 months, as consumers move on to the next trend.

Long-term trends: 5 years

A trend that lasts around 5 years would be classed as long-term. Trends that last longer than a few seasons tend to focus on certain key items whose form develops over time, such as high heels with hidden (or overlasted) platforms. These became higher and spikier between their launch (the 1.2-inch platform of the YSL Tribute shoe in 2007) and the sky-high 2.5-inch platforms of 2011.

These tend to be the trends that mark out an era and eventually become essential for consumers who want to look modern. They are 'slow burn' trends that consumers may buy into in several different ways, for example by owning several pairs of skinny jeans or different styles of platform shoes.

Opposite, left to right: Model Agyness Deyn in Dr Martens boots, which she helped to become a long-term trend; School playgrounds create, and kill, many fads, such as animal-shaped rubber wrist bands Silly Bandz.

Classics: 10–25 years

A classic is a look or item that has mass appeal and utility, and is often regarded as a modern 'essential' – an article that most people own in some form or another. In fashion terms, this could mean a key garment such as a trench coat, 'little black dress' or pair of jeans. And while classics are fairly continuously produced, sold and used, they evolve to suit each era. For example, the shape and colour of jeans changes according to current fashion, from flares, bootcuts and skinnies to snow-wash, coloured and torn styles.

Long-term trends can evolve into classics. One recent example is the omnipresent skinny jean, which was first seen as a cutting-edge fashion item; however, its comfort and adaptability have turned it into a new classic, worn by people of all genders, ages and backgrounds.

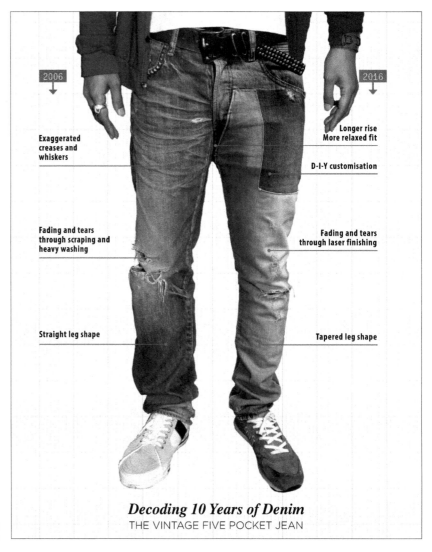

2006

Exaggerated
creases and
whiskers

Fading and tears
through scraping and
heavy washing

Straight leg shape

2016

Longer rise
More relaxed fit

D-I-Y customisation

Fading and tears
through laser finishing

Tapered leg shape

Decoding 10 Years of Denim
THE VINTAGE FIVE POCKET JEAN

Even classic items, such as blue denim jeans, evolve over the years. Graphic by View2 *magazine illustrating the small changes in jean styles for men over a 10-year period.*

Limiters

All of these factors can have a positive or negative effect on trends – too much or too little can overexpose a trend or restrict it to niche status.

* *Celebrity adoption/recommendation (e.g. Kim Kardashian's adoption of peplums, which caused a spike in interest of the silhouette).*

* *New brands (e.g. Vetements' popularity fuelling trends for frayed denim and ironic branded T-shirts).*

* *Media discussion. Outrage about, or support for, particular trends in the media can promote or prevent the growth of trends, such as super-sheer red-carpet gowns.*

* *Immediate friends and family. The attitudes and beliefs of those around you can prevent or promote the purchase of certain items, or ways of dressing. For example, a conservative social group may discourage adventurous garments or styling.*

* *Appearance in culture. An example is Rouge Noir nail polish; sales boomed after it was reportedly worn by Uma Thurman's character in* Pulp Fiction.

* *Availability – too much (saturation) or too little (scarcity).*

Fake designer bags. Fashionable bag designs, or 'It bags' are much sought after and widely copied, but fake versions can limit the growth of the trend for that bag.

Trend cycle

There are only so many new ideas in fashion, so trends tend to move in cycles that can last many years. This is partly due to the nature of fashion – always looking for new ideas and new kinds of beauty. A look that is the ultimate in style one year can be highly unfashionable just a few years later, making those people who still wear that look (or still try to sell it) seem dated or backward. But, many years later, that trend may return again with a new vigour and a new way of being worn – such as shoulder pads, which were worn in power suits during the 1980s, but returned in the 2000s in the form of body-conscious occasionwear. This is the trend cycle.

Trend forecasters must monitor how trends fade and return to ensure that they are ahead of the cycle, not behind it. Here, we will explore the cycle of key trends, and how retro inspirations return every couple of decades.

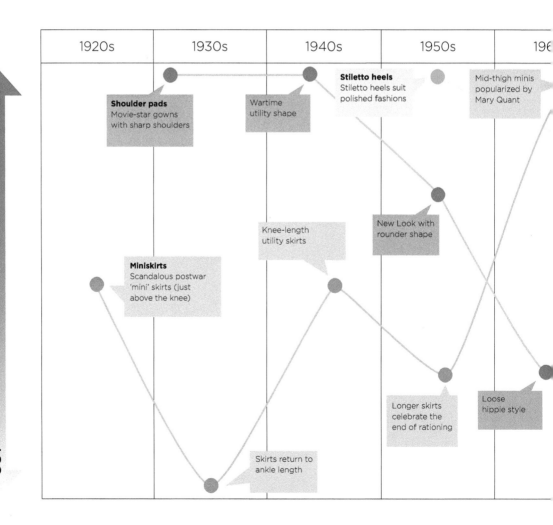

The defining look of key eras tends to come round again about 20 years afterwards – for example the 1980s-influenced fashions of the 2000s or the return of both 1990s minimalism and grunge in the 2010s.

There are several theories as to why this happens. Some suggest that because 20 years is the standard gap between generations, young people are inspired by the clothes that looked cool on their parents at the same age. It could also be about nostalgia for lifestyles of that era, or referencing earlier decades as a way of understanding the current era – such as invoking the upbeat hippie style of late 1960s flower children during late 1980s and early 1990s rave culture (known as the 'second summer of love').

Others argue that it takes around 20 years for a style to cycle through the stages of being popular, overexposed, then unfashionable and forgotten, until it is rediscovered and adopted by a new generation.

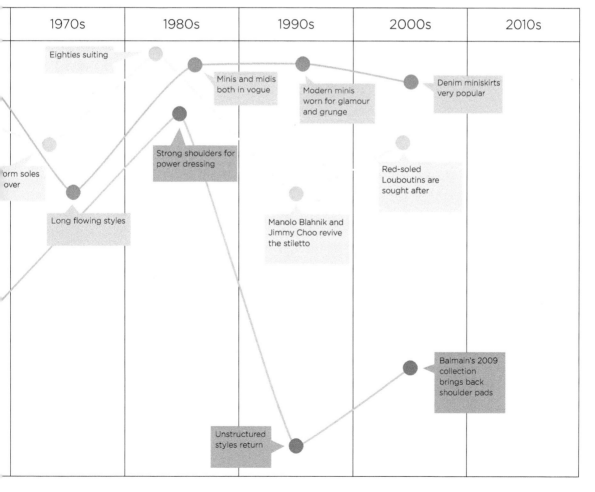

| 1970s | 1980s | 1990s | 2000s | 2010s |

Eighties suiting

Minis and midis both in vogue

Modern minis worn for glamour and grunge

Denim miniskirts very popular

Strong shoulders for power dressing

orm soles over

Red-soled Louboutins are sought after

Long flowing styles

Manolo Blahnik and Jimmy Choo revive the stiletto

Balmain's 2009 collection brings back shoulder pads

Unstructured styles return

Trend influencers

Trends don't just spring up from nowhere – they emerge from multiple ideas and pieces of information, and are fostered and developed by key influencers such as fashion professionals or pop-culture icons. These can influence the life cycles of a trend, as well as the audience for it.

Trend influencers have changed from royalty and ultra-wealthy society figures to designers, celebrities, and now street-style stars (refer to Chapter 1 for more detail on historical influencers, and p.62 for changing influencers). Here, we explore how different influences, from street style to high fashion, can help shape a trend.

Until fairly recently, the key influencers of trends were skilled industry professionals – those who create or disseminate new products for a living, travelling the world to keep up with what is happening where (see 'Traditional influencers', below). The lists below are not exhaustive, but include some of the key figures who help turn an idea into a trend, by visualizing, spreading or embodying it. According to Rogers' diffusion-of-innovation model, these are the innovators and early adopters who kick-start a trend.

Traditional influencers
* Stylists
* Editors
* Writers
* Designers
* Retailers
* Celebrities
* Costume designers
* Models

New influencers
* Street-style stars
* Bloggers and other social-media stars
* Creative consumers

Front row, Burberry Autumn/Winter 2012. Celebrities now join fashion professionals on the front row of catwalk shows. Left to right, will.i.am, Alexa Chung, Jeremy Irvine, Clémence Poésy, Eddie Redmayne, Rosie Huntington-Whiteley, Mario Testino, Kate Bosworth and Michael Polish.

The red-carpet effect

The celebrities who walk the red carpet, and those who dress and style them, are increasingly influential when it comes to trends. Occasionwear, in particular, takes many cues from red-carpet style, but details such as necklines, colour, embellishment and silhouette can influence other product categories, too.

Social media, fashion blogs and press coverage of movie premieres, arts events and awards ceremonies help to showcase the gowns and tailoring worn by celebrities, which can inspire consumers and designers alike. A few moments on the red carpet can help spread the appeal of designers' creations that would not otherwise be visible to the average consumer.

Many brands now regard the red carpet as a key way to publicize their designs – and their brand name. Every year, hundreds of millions of people across the globe watch award ceremonies in Hollywood and Bollywood, for the fashion as much as the awards.

'The cinema and the media in general have a strong impact on the public: People identify with celebrities, who influence their choices on what to wear. The [red-carpet-to-retail connection] stems from the aura associated with the star, with which the public identifies. Over the years, in fact, we have had several requests for dresses identical to those on the red carpet, which confirms that my job, even for the stars, is never a style exercise or an end in itself, but is based on a solid and real idea. After George Clooney's wedding, for example, we registered an increase in requests for three-piece suits similar to the one he wore during the ceremony.'
Giorgio Armani, quoted on WWD.com, February 2015

Remember, however, that while the clothes seen on celebrities are highly influential, they rarely select these garments themselves, but have pieces chosen for them by an experienced fashion professional – a stylist.

Changing trend influencers

The people who influence trends – and the ways that they influence them – are now changing. While many trends still 'trickle down' from traditional influencers to the rest of the population, it is equally likely that trends are originated by consumers themselves and end up influencing high fashion ('bubble-up' trends). Here, we explore how trends spread from traditional or new influencers to the rest of the market.

Trickle-down theory

Affluent, well-connected 'elite' consumers buy into the latest products, and their glamorous, aspirational lifestyles inspire lower-social-class consumers to copy them with cheaper versions of key trends. In order to remain elite, affluent consumers differentiate themselves by buying into new fashions, which poorer consumers cannot yet afford (but will eventually copy). In this way, the trends adopted by those at the top of the social order trickle down different market levels to influence what those at the bottom will wear.

The trickle-down effect

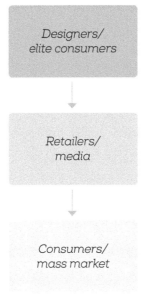

Princess Diana in 1995. Elites, such as royalty, celebrities and other wealthy consumers, have traditionally led trends, as they can afford to keep buying and trying new fashions. These fashions are then emulated by fashion professionals and retailers, to be consumed by the mass market.

Bubble-up theory

Designers and fashion influencers are also inspired by niche groups, styles and subcultures, and help bring their aesthetic to the masses – bubbling up from the underground to the mainstream and the catwalk. Also known as trickle-up theory, this idea suggests that those 'at the bottom' influence those 'higher up'. Researching subcultures and niche groups has been a popular way for designers to find inspiration for many years, with Yves Saint Laurent's 1966 Rive Gauche collection, which was influenced by the style of beatniks on Paris' Left Bank, being one of the most famous. Other designers have taken inspiration from non-mainstream worlds such as club culture, underground music scenes, indigenous tribes, youth subcultures and extreme sports.

Adopting from subcultures or style tribes wholesale rarely works commercially, but forecasters can spot the growing influence of these groups through niche media and artists as well as elements of their style (clothing/styling/accessories/brands) being adopted by young people or in street style.

The bubble-up effect

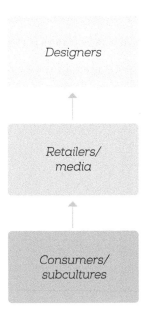

Stylish consumers – often seen in street style images – and members of style tribes can kick-start trends that are then taken up by retailers and designer fashion brands.

Trickle-across theory

Rather than trends spreading from the top downwards over time, or from the bottom upwards, trickle-across theory suggests that trends are available at all levels of the market simultaneously. Trickle-across trends occur when a trend can be adapted for multiple price points and types of consumer. A recent example might be the pastel-pink winter coat of 2013/14 that emerged as a key item on catwalks, but hit stores at designer, mid-market and fast-fashion levels at the same time, meaning that whatever their budget any consumer could buy into the trend. Trickle-across trends have become increasingly common since it became more acceptable for mainstream retailers to create their own versions of key designer pieces in the 1930s.

Trickle-across trends

Catwalk trends

Designer stores ←→ Middle market ←→ Fast fashion

Trends for Timberland work boots have proliferated across all levels of the market simultaneously, being taken up by designer brands, consumers and celebrities at the same time.

New ecosystem

While trickle-down, bubble-up and trickle-across trends are still common, it is now more difficult to dictate which way trends will develop. Democratized fashion and online media mean that a trend can start at the mid-market and spread outwards to the top and bottom ends, or go direct from a subculture to a luxury brand without ever hitting the mainstream.

Key fashion trends are also less dominant now than in previous decades, with consumers less willing to adopt a single style than they were in the past (such as the 'brown is the new black' diktat). As a result, the path of a trend is not always clear-cut, and certain trends may exist only at one level of the market while others will hit different strata at different times, making many trends more of an ecosystem than a simple flow chart.

New ecosystem: traditional (left) vs. contemporary flow (right)

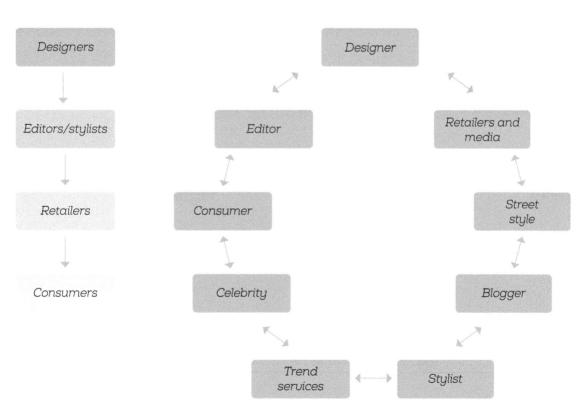

Industry profile
Aki Choklat

Biography

Aki Choklat is an internationally acclaimed leading fashion and footwear design professional with a breadth of experience across the fashion industry, from design to production. A Royal College of Art graduate, Choklat is the director of his own footwear label, a design and trend consultant with varied clients from Harley-Davidson, Caterpillar and Puma to Chalhoub, and a leading Middle Eastern luxury retailer. He also wrote the Master in Fashion Trend Forecasting program at Polimoda, Italy, which he led for five years. Currently Aki is Chair and Associate Professor of Fashion Accessories Design at the College for Creative Studies in Detroit, US, where he has incorporated trend thinking into the curriculum.

How do you approach trend research and the forecasting process?

My approach to trend research is very intuitive. I try not to be too systematic in the beginning, preferring keeping myself open. I look more at the bigger cultural phenomena to understand the direction we are going in as a society. Ultimately what we want to understand is the consumption pattern of people before they do it.

Do you have a methodology?

Yes. I always start with writing down words and drawing some ideas I have seen. I travel so much between my post in the US, business based in Europe and lecturing that I am constantly seeing interesting things. I go through several notebooks every year and review when it is time to filter the information. So I start from observing culture, filtering information and cross-referencing to see if there is a path that can evolve into a trend.

Which sectors of the industry do you find most inspiring for your work, be they social, cultural or aesthetic?

I do love just about everything about the fashion industry. I like the raw materials shows to understand innovation and what direction production will go. I love street style and photograph interesting people with personal style. I like the democracy of it. I also analyse pretty much every catwalk show, possible not only as a trend professional but also as a fashion enthusiast.

What trend forecasting services do you use, either professionally or personally?

I love Copenhagen Institute for Futures Studies and The Future Laboratory, since they both have very good free content on their channels. Of course WGSN is the mother-ship which I use for getting a global retail understanding and Trendstop (where I continue to work as consultant) for consumer-driven trends.

How do you think the usage of trends is changing for the fashion industry?

Trend agencies used to be in a strong position because they helped companies to understand better what direction to take. Now there is so much information online that many industries can do it themselves. I think this is a big problem since professional assistance is needed now more than ever. Many fashion houses blindly download trend reports and pin them on the boards and design based on that feed. I do not think that is how to do it ... trends offer great inspiration but how to translate the information is more difficult.

What is the single thing no trend forecaster can be without?

A notebook to document your experiences. You are the best browser there is.

What inspires you most?

Creative people. Musicians, makers, writers ... people that do things I cannot do. Also, people that do good inspire me. In design and fashion I love meeting young minds and innovators. I also get inspired by cities and all that they have to offer. Tokyo inspires me.

What tools – website, blog, book, place, object – can you not be without?
I have an extensive reading list but the usual readings are a must from Georg Simmel, Thorstein Veblen, Walter Benjamin to Everett Rogers and Richard Dawkins. For more current reading I do like fashion magazines such as *Garage* and *Vogue Italia*. I do try to get hold of all the cult Japanese magazines such as *Popeye* and *Free & Easy*. For visuals I love *Volt* and am crazy about *Plethora Magazine*. For websites SHOWstudio, obviously, but also khole.net and DIS Magazine.com.

How did you end up in trend forecasting?
After I graduated from the RCA my first job was a forecasting job at a London agency, Bureaux, who worked with *View Magazine* and had international clients. They were looking for a footwear specialist and contacted me. It was my first trend gig and I absolutely loved it.

What advice would you give to someone who wants to get involved in forecasting?
Study social sciences as much if not even more than fashion and the culture of fashion. If you love the beauty of fashion but do not want to be a designer, but you also love the business of fashion but do not want to be a business analyst, trend forecasting is a good path in the middle to consider.

The rise of the blogger

The flow of fashion information is evolving, giving consumers and non-professionals a voice. The most visible shift in consumer-driven fashion influence has been the rise of the fashion blogger. Since individuals began to document their personal style online, in about 2004, these tech- and media-savvy mavens have become increasingly influential. Their 'outsider's view' has come to resonate better with fashion consumers than the exclusive outlook of traditional fashion magazines.

Armed with a blog, a camera, a keen sense of personal style and a love of fashion, bloggers gave their unvarnished opinions on fashion brands, media and products. In the process, they attracted millions of readers worldwide, who were attracted by their honest and witty take on fashion and trends. Bloggers began to escape industry derision once brands realized how influential they were to their fans, who would snap up their favourite bloggers' latest recommendations and 'obsessions'. Products that are featured by bloggers as 'must-haves' can quickly sell out, and they can spur trends based purely on their own interests.

Bloggers have now become part of the modern fashion establishment, bringing their readers into the closed ranks of the fashion industry and creating a powerful new trend influence as a result. Leading bloggers are now courted by key designers and attend many of the events previously reserved for 'insiders'.

Leandra Medine, influential fashion blogger, and creator of the popular website Man Repeller.

EXERCISE: TRACK A TREND'S EVOLUTION

Using the basic trend skills detailed in this chapter, track the evolution of a trend. Choose a colour, key item or styling trend and monitor how it evolves from an idea to a fully realized trend. Find visual examples of your trend in offline and online media, and analyse the direction of the trend – is it growing or waning?

These sources can help you track a trend

* Articles in magazines, newspapers or blogs.
* People you know, people you see on the street, or people you follow on social media.
* TV shows, music videos, exhibitions, movies.
* Red-carpet coverage, celebrity style.

Use magazine cuttings and other physical sources to create a trend-tracking board, or you can use digital bookmarks or even a Tumblr blog to save all your references in one place.

Research how a current trend has evolved

* Where did the trend start?
* How has it evolved?
* Who are the key influencers?
* Has the trend bubbled up, or trickled down or across?
* Do you think this is a fad, a seasonal or long-term trend – or even a classic?
* Consider why this trend has become popular.
* Which group is currently fostering the trend (early majority/laggards, etc.)?

Observe how a current idea evolves into a future trend

* Look out for an item, colour combination or style that seems interesting, unusual or new to you.
* Make a note of where you see this idea appearing – street style, social media, catwalks, stores, magazines, red carpet.
* Where is the idea coming from – traditional influencers or new influencers?
* How is the idea evolving into a full trend?
* Consider what factors might affect whether this trend becomes more popular.
* Which group is currently fostering the trend (innovators/ early adopters, etc.)?

Once you are confident that you can identify how a trend has evolved, you can now apply your skills to observing one as it evolves in real time.

ELEPHANT

HOW TO MAKE A DENT
IN THE UNIVERSE

smith
JOURNAL

PORT

Dansk

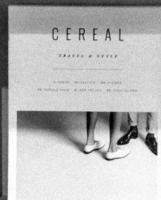

CEREAL

TRAVEL & STYLE

KINFOLK

oh comely

It's spring!

RE-EDITION

wehaveeverything & wehavenothing

LOVE CLUB

LILY ROSE
DEPP

'I wanted something calm.'

4

Trend Research

This chapter explores how you can look for ideas and inspiration – where to find what is new and next, how to monitor the zeitgeist and look for trends at their nascent stages.

The focus shifts from the theory of trends and how the industry works, towards practical ways to start trend research, manage ideas and tap into your instincts. We will look at the key areas of research, from pop culture to technology. We will also look at primary and secondary research, and the importance of personal participation and the experience of physical objects. Good trend ideas tend to come from diverse sources and methods of research, so we encourage you to take a lateral approach to your research – you never know where the next good idea will come from.

Just as important as doing research is managing your sources and ideas, so that you can retrieve or reference them later. This chapter details some of the key physical and digital methods for managing the ideas you have collected.

Fashion and design magazines are a great starting point for images and ideas for trend research.

Research

This section looks at the what, why and where of finding information to inform and inspire a trend, such as what is happening in popular culture, design, entertainment and lifestyle.

Getting started

Start by setting up a bank of sources that you can check regularly for inspiration and ideas. Look for media, places and websites that you enjoy, which have great information or visuals, or just a unique viewpoint. The categories and sources on the following pages will help to start your research.

Do not limit yourself to fashion sources. The strongest trends are based on a broad range of well-considered and often esoteric sources, so the first step should be to look beyond the world of fashion. Otherwise, you will just be recreating what is happening in the marketplace, not pushing it forwards – which is, after all, the aim of trend forecasting.

THINK LATERALLY WHEN SEARCHING ONLINE. VISIT YOUR FAVOURED SOURCES, BUT ALSO FOLLOW RELATED LINKS OR READ RELATED STORIES TO FIND NEW WELLSPRINGS OF INSPIRATION. IT IS ALSO WORTH EXPLORING SPECIALIST MEDIA AND WEBSITES THAT ARE RELATED TO YOUR LINE OF ENQUIRY, SUCH AS SCIENCE JOURNALS OR PRODUCT WEBSITES.

Right: Gucci Cruise 2017 fashion show in the cloisters of Westminster Abbey, London.

Opposite: Magazine tearsheets can be a useful source of ideas.

Fashion

What

If you are working towards a fashion-trend forecast, creating a roster of fashion sources can be an easy way in to the research process, whether by looking at fashion magazines (from niche to mainstream), watching or viewing images from catwalk shows, or attending collection previews and trunk shows.

Why

If you are having trouble distilling your ideas into a workable product direction, reviewing fashion sources can help to bring a dose of reality, but more often it is about keeping abreast with what is happening in the industry so that you are on top of – if not ahead of – fashion trends.

Where

Attend catwalk shows, if possible. The live buzz of a show can give you an idea of which designs are resonating most with press and buyers.

* Watch live-streamed catwalk shows or videos.

* Follow catwalk sites, such as catwalking.com or imaxtree.com, which offer close-ups of key materials, details, accessories and beauty.

* Look at fashion-trend services.

* Read catwalk coverage on mainstream press or consumer fashion sites such as style.com.

* Keep abreast of media – fashion magazines, whether trade or consumer – that can help give you an idea of key looks and how current trends are being received.

* Follow key fashion influencers such as editors, stylists and bloggers on social media to get instant coverage and opinion on key collections and styles.

Rodarte's Autumn/Winter 2014 collection was influenced by the original Star Wars *movies.*

Popular culture

What

For mainstream or fast-fashion brands in particular, it is important to stay on top of what is happening in pop culture. Which are the musicians, celebrities, films, TV shows and events that everyone is talking about? These inform the zeitgeist that, in turn, informs the shape and progress of trends (see Chapter 1, pp.16–19).

Why

New entertainment can be particularly influential (blockbuster TV shows; *Game of Thrones*, *Mad Men*), as well as revivals or re-releases (*Star Wars*, *Blade Runner*). Films, in particular, have long influenced fashion, such as the impact of the 1986 hockey film *Youngblood* on Stuart Vevers' Autumn/Winter 2016/2017 collection for Coach. The film may be inspiring or influential because of its costume design, production design, cinematography or just its message. Films are also planned many years in advance (much like exhibitions), and so help shape the zeitgeist.

Where

* Magazine covers.
* Social-media 'buzz'.
* Watercooler chat.
* Mainstream-media coverage.
* Cinema and events such as film festivals.

CULTIVATING SPECIALIST SOURCES FOR YOUR MARKET AND FOLLOWING THEM, OR KNOWING WHO TO LOOK AT, KEEPS YOU WELL INFORMED AND ABLE TO RESPOND TO NEARLY ANY BRIEF.

FOR EXAMPLE, AN OCCASIONWEAR DESIGNER MAY LOOK AT COUTURE, BRIDALWEAR AND THE WEDDING MARKET, CELEBRITIES, RED-CARPET STREET SHOTS AND LUXURY FABRIC AND MATERIAL TRADE SHOWS.

A MENSWEAR DESIGNER MAY LOOK AT DENIM, SAVILE ROW BESPOKE TAILORS, CELEBRITIES, SPORTS PERSONALITIES, MUSIC CULTURE, RETAIL, FOOD AND DRINK, TECHNOLOGY AND ARCHITECTURE.

Street style

What

Street style is increasingly influential within fashion – especially when it comes to trends in styling, youth culture, denim and activewear. The way that fashion professionals, bloggers (see p.33) and other stylish professionals put together an outfit can kick-start new styling trends, as well as demonstrating which brands and designs are capturing the interest of early adopters. Fashion weeks offer a wealth of street style, but many blogs, magazines and websites track street style all year round – among them sites such as The Sartorialist and the regular coverage by services such as WGSN.

Why

Fashion events are not the only place to look out for inspiring ideas and styling. Events such as music festivals can spark ideas for casual and occasion fashion, while attendees at art and design events (see 'Arts', p.78) offer more directional styling inspiration.

Subculture members, such as fans of a particular music genre, or those living a particular lifestyle, tend to have an influence on trends since they are early adopters or even the originators of a key look that may filter into the mass consciousness over time.

Where

* Street-style blogs.
* Personal style blogs.
* Instagram and Tumblr.

* Fashion press – digital and in print.
* Trend services – WGSN, Trendstop, etc. (see Chapter 2, pp.38–39).

Outside Tokyo Fashion Week for Autumn/Winter 2017. Street-style shots can inspire new styling ideas, as well as helping to spotlight new brands and trends.

House of Hackney store, London.
Innovative retail stores can offer
ideas for new products as well as
showcasing new brands and design.

Retail

What

Retail research such as comp shopping can be a great way to check how different brands and designers are approaching a key trend, as well as offering new ideas and observing which trends are selling well.

Why

As retail is the last point in the trend process, retail research tends to be more useful for confirming a trend than for researching new ones, but seeking out boutiques and specialist stores that may have more unusual stock can spark new ideas and routes for research.

Where

* On the street. Check out new stores, key shopping streets and up-and-coming neighbourhoods.

* Data trend services such as TrendAnalytics, Edited and WGSN InStock.

* Fashion trade press, e.g. *Drapers*, *WWD*, *Retail Week*, *Sportswear International*, *Footwear News*.

IT IS VITAL THAT WHEN SEARCHING THROUGH INFLUENCES FOR SUITABLE MATERIAL YOU MAKE SURE THAT ALL YOUR SOURCES ARE NOTED, SAVED OR BOOKMARKED – BOTH FOR ATTRIBUTION PURPOSES AND FOR FUTURE REFERENCE. THAT WAY, YOU CAN BUILD UP A LARGE BODY OF VALUABLE SOURCES ACROSS A RANGE OF SUBJECTS THAT CAN BE USED QUICKLY AND EASILY. THIS PRACTICE ALSO ENABLES YOU TO GATHER IDEAS ON AN ONGOING BASIS, IN ORDER TO KEEP YOURSELF UP TO DATE WITH WHAT IS GOING ON AND WHERE.

Design

What
Design covers a wide swathe of skills and industry, from architecture and product design to interiors, furniture, graphics and even appliances.

Why
Designers often experiment with new materials and forms that can inspire fashion trends. They can also offer new ways of thinking about space, shape and silhouette to inspire fashion designers' work.

Product design
New products are launched constantly. Trade shows offer a good opportunity to see materials, colours, shapes and new styles before they hit the shops or are even picked up by retailers.

Architecture
Building design can have a big influence on the fashion industry. Fashion designers such as Hussein Chalayan, Issey Miyake and Dice Kayek are inspired by architectural proportions, scale and engineering.

Where
* Design sites – Dezeen, Designboom, It's Nice That.

* Trade shows and fairs – Salone del Mobile in Milan; MAISON&OBJET in Paris, Asia and the Americas; London Design Festival; International Design Expo in Eindhoven.

* Design magazines – *Eye*, *Elle Decoration*, *Frame*.

* Exhibitions – Cooper Hewitt, New York; Design Museum Holon, Israel; Centre de Cultura Contemporània de Barcelona (CCCB); Design Museum, London; Helsinki Design Museum.

* Retail research – see which trends are featured in shop windows, on mannequins, or promoted through websites or brand newsletters.

The Flötotto stand at Salone del Mobile, Milan, 2015.

Arts

What

The arts are a broad sector but hugely important for offering inspiration, not only because you can engage with other forms of creativity but also because other creators can inform your own work. Key areas to explore from a trends perspective are contemporary art, theatre and dance.

Why

The arts – especially visual arts – have long influenced designers and trends alike. The relationship between fashion and art is a strong one, with some designers using artworks to inspire their creations, such as Yves Saint Laurent's famous Mondrian dress.

Where

Exhibitions are perhaps the easiest – and most enjoyable – way to immerse yourself in new ideas. Check out both the big shows and influential galleries in any city you visit. New and established artists can offer fresh ways of thinking about colour, texture and mood. Furthermore, key exhibitions can prove especially influential for design, culture and the zeitgeist. Exhibition schedules are published years in advance, and so can be a useful gauge of what will be influencing popular culture for the season you are considering. For example, the Rara Avis exhibition at New York's Metropolitan Museum of Art in 2005 launched Iris Apfel as a global style icon, as well as shaking up ideas about how older women can and should dress.

Iris Apfel putting the finishing touches to an exhibition of her style, Rara Avis: Selections from the Iris Apfel Collection in 2005. The show helped turn the then 84-year-old New Yorker into a style icon.

Fairs
The Armory Show in New York; Art Basel in Basel, Hong Kong and Miami Beach; Frieze London; Venice Biennale.

Theatre
Writers often have a unique viewpoint on how we live and what we want that can prompt new ways of thinking. Often, experimental theatres or companies work with equally experimental set, music and costume designers, who can also offer new levels of inspiration.

Books
Upcoming and new books by art publishers can open up new visual worlds, from in-depth explorations of artists' work to compendiums of underground talent and undiscovered or indigenous arts.

Dance
Contemporary or experimental dance ensembles, such as the Michael Clark Company and the Hofesh Shechter Company, can offer new perspectives on movement and the body.

Left to right: The Michael Clark Company performing at the Glastonbury Festival, 2015; Kenyan Cyrus Kabiru's eyewear sculptures are a metaphor for the change of view needed today in relation to Africa.

From Making Africa: A Continent of Contemporary Design exhibition, in collaboration with Amunga Eshuchi, as seen at Centre de Cultura Contemporània de Barcelona in 2016.

Lifestyle

What

Stay at the cutting edge of changes in how people travel, socialize, and spend their time and money by tracking consumer lifestyle trends. Global consumer-trend services offer regular feeds of new shifts in consumer behaviour and lifestyle, which can be especially useful for their sections on key demographics (such as millennials or boomers) and sectors (such as luxury and travel). Good trend researchers, however, can do much of this work for themselves. You can monitor mainstream media, for example, to understand the zeitgeist and the market into which your trend will emerge.

Why

This kind of information can be especially useful for informing macro trends or background research, providing the context for your trend. Lifestyle categories include health and wellness, beauty, travel, automotive, sports and leisure – all of which can provide ideas for your next project. Lifestyle research gives the 'big picture' element to fashion forecasts, and can add depth – which, in turn, makes your trend more robust.

Where

* Expert talks – TED Talks, Do Lectures, creative symposia.

* Agencies, companies and websites – LS:N Global, Protein, PSFK, the Cassandra Report, Stylus, Faith Popcorn's Brain Reserve.

* Broadsheet newspapers (in print or online).

* Radio – NPR, BBC Radio 4.

* News and current-affairs magazines – *Time*, *The Economist*, *Atlantic*, *New Republic*, *New Yorker*.

Food and drink

What

Food and drink have become increasingly influential within a social context, with interest in food origin, styling and experiences exploding in recent years.

Why

Food and drink can give insight into people's priorities and aspirations, and also offer a wealth of ideas around texture, colour, surface and mood.

Where

* New restaurants.

* Magazines – *Kinfolk*, *Lucky Peach*.

* Social media, especially Pinterest and Instagram.

Monument Valley *game by UsTwo.*

Digital culture and technology

What

The ways in which we work and entertain ourselves are increasingly digital. Gaming, in particular, is emerging as an influence on trends – whether in terms of aesthetics (like *Monument Valley*) or the game's message itself (for example, *Mountain* or *Depression Quest*).

By looking at new ways of using the Internet and social media, gaming and new technologies – from mainstream devices, such as smartphones, to progressive ideas like virtual reality (VR) headsets, exoskeletons and artificial intelligence (AI) – we can keep ideas moving forward.

Why

Arguably, digital culture *is* culture nowadays, as we live more of our lives online; certain aesthetics, tribes, behaviours and ideas live almost exclusively online. The digital industries are constantly innovating and can lead you into new ideas of what is possible in terms of form and function.

Where

* Research institutes – MIT Media Lab, the Royal College of Art.

* Tech-focused media – Wired, TechCrunch, The Mary Sue, Gizmodo websites.

* Tech industry events – the Consumer Electronics Show (CES), SXSW Interactive, Lift Conference, E3 Expo gaming conference, Mobile World Congress, Digital-Life-Design.

Imagery

In trend forecasting, imagery is a crucial ingredient. It is a visual synopsis of the elements that go into the trend, and helps the viewer to understand the references behind the trend as well as the general feeling it imparts. You should be able to understand what the trend is generally about, who it is aimed at and what it is saying with a quick glance at a mood board.

See Chapter 5 for the wide variety of sources from which images can be gleaned, such as magazines, books, websites, blogs, photographers, artists, fashion and design shoots, product images, press releases and personal photography.

ONGOING RESEARCH IS ESSENTIAL TO TREND FORECASTING, AS IT ALLOWS YOU TO BETTER READ HOW TRENDS ARE EMERGING. YOU MAY CHOOSE TO SPEND A LITTLE TIME EVERY DAY TO ADD TO, AND PROGRESS, YOUR RESEARCH, OR SEVERAL HOURS ONCE A WEEK. RESEARCHING ANY LESS OFTEN THAN WEEKLY COULD MAKE IT DIFFICULT TO GET A TRUE UNDERSTANDING OF HOW TRENDS ARE DEVELOPING.

OF COURSE, YOU MAY HAVE LAST-MINUTE OR AD HOC PROJECTS WHICH TAKE YOU OUT OF THE REALMS OF YOUR EXISTING RESEARCH, WHICH IS WHY IT IS IMPORTANT TO HAVE A SUITE OF INNOVATIVE BUT RELIABLE SOURCES ON HAND SO THAT YOU CAN IMMERSE YOURSELF IN NEW CATEGORIES IF NECESSARY.

Left: A trend table from the Heimtextil trade fair. Well-selected imagery helps to illustrate the trend idea.

Right: A mood board of inspiring images at the beginning of the trend research process.

Lethabo Tsatsinyane photographed for Dazed *magazine by Chris Saunders, 2010. International trend trips can open your mind to new print, pattern, colour and silhouette – as well as new ideas.*

Cultivating curiosity

A good trend forecaster needs to be adept at researching and spotting patterns, but the key characteristic of great trend forecasters is boundless curiosity.

Not everyone is naturally, relentlessly curious, but it is something you can cultivate by learning to appreciate the thrill of the new. For a trend forecaster, the idea that 'you do not know what you do not know' is liberating – it means you do not yet know where your ideas could take you. And that can be very exciting.

Everything around you can influence your trends, and, ultimately, everything you do, see, hear and experience can be research.

* *Start by ranging widely – get inspired.*

* *Spot patterns in what you have found.*

* *Look everywhere – observe, consider, 'connect the dots' and use intuition.*

* *Be willing to follow your ideas wherever they take you, and to listen.*

* *Start with an open mind – you never know where ideas and inspiration will come from.*

* *Embrace discovery.*

Do not see research as an arduous task, but as a new way of tuning your mind to pick up on the unusual, the new and the extraordinary, as well as noticing subtle shifts in the zeitgeist.

THERE IS A LOT OF 'CHAFF' IN THE TREND PROCESS, AND THAT IS OKAY. GET USED TO COLLECTING THINGS THAT INTEREST YOU, AND PUTTING IDEAS TOGETHER IN DIFFERENT WAYS AS YOU DEVELOP YOUR CONCEPTS. SOME OBJECTS OR OBSERVATIONS MAY GO UNUSED FOR MANY WEEKS OR MONTHS, AND SOME MAY NEVER BE USED AT ALL.

Instinct and intuition

Alongside the process of research and analysis, gut feeling and intuition are crucial to formulating a trend. The ideas that inform trends can be taken in subconsciously, and often the collective subconscious is what cements a trend.

Intuition cannot be taught, but everyone has it to some degree – you just have to learn to listen to it. That flutter that happens when you find something new? That moment where you find yourself exploring an idea, subject, person, product or place you had never thought about before? That 'ping' when you realize that the thing you are looking at reminds you of something else you have seen? That is your instinct at work.

Your intuition needs ideas, so absorb as many new and unusual places, ideas and experiences as you can. Get your mind active, and your instincts will come alive too. Delve into the categories listed above, and look out for that flutter when you find a person, category or product that really captures your attention. If you find yourself revisiting certain websites, artists or industries, for example, that suggests you have found an area that particularly inspires you – so make sure to explore it.

It is important to learn what works for you, which is why different methods and sources are detailed here. Finding inspiration can be tricky, so it is important to understand your own way of working and what inspires you – then work with it, not against it.

If there are magazines that you like – get a subscription. Websites you like – sign up to the newsletter. People who interest you – follow them on social media.

Ask yourself:
* Is this new?
* How is it different?
* What about it interests me?

EXERCISE:
SET UP SOURCES

Trend forecasting is based on strong research skills. By setting up a bank of sources that you can check regularly, you can ensure your research is not only contemporary, but future-forward. It will also allow you to respond quickly to new briefs.

* *Research interesting, inspiring and influential sources for each of the categories on pp. 73–81.*

* *Start by checking out sources you are already familiar with.*

* *Ask friends and colleagues where they get their inspiration from, or if they have read, seen or experienced something interesting lately.*

* *Think about which articles or magazines you have read that intrigued you.*

* *Create bookmarks for blogs, Tumblrs or websites you have found recently.*

* *Follow key people and institutions on social media.*

* *Look at different platforms – online and printed media, TV and film, exhibitions and the arts – and check out new venues in your neighbourhood.*

* *Ensure you have a mixture of mainstream sources (such as newspapers and fashion magazines) as well as more cutting-edge or specialist ones.*

* *Check online sources several times a week.*

* *Try to spot patterns in interesting things you find from different sources. This is the beginning of building a trend.*

WeWork offices in London. WeWork is a worldwide network of office spaces for freelancers to use.

Industry profile
Louise Byg Kongsholm

Biography
Louise Byg Kongsholm is the owner and director of Scandinavian trend company Pej Gruppen, which creates seasonal colour, material and design directions, as well as acting as an agent for other trend services from WGSN, Trend Union, Nelly Rodi, Mode...Information and Pantone. She has a background in retail and brand consultancy for leading European brands and retailers and has authored several books on trends and sociology.

How did you get started in trends?
Pej Gruppen was founded in 1975 by my father and I guess I was always a part of the family business. I took a master's degree in strategy and management and worked for several years at Lego, but decided to give the family business a go in 2007 and bought it in 2011. So depending on how you look at it, I have been in the trend business my entire life or only since 2007.

What is your research process?
Our basis is always the current and future zeitgeist, consumer behaviour across generations and a deep understanding of the different types of trends (giga, mega, micro and fads) and then interpreting that into category and seasonal trends. The process is longer than most people expect, but the results are so much more accurate.

What do clients need from a trend forecast?
Most clients are looking for a sense of direction and are constantly trying to get it just right. The amount of trend inspiration out there – both offline and online – has increased dramatically and as a consequence we see our role as the provider of secure, commercial and filtered trend forecasts for the Scandinavian markets.

What do you and your clients find to be the most effective way of presenting trend ideas?
Clients are very different when it comes to the right way of getting across the trends, feeling, mood, stories, colours and materials. Some want text, others only visuals. We find that a combination of several communicative tools is most successful; we use text, key words, collages, colours and colour combinations along with presentations with short films as inspiration.

What advice would you give to someone starting out in trends now?
Be absolutely sure that you know what you are doing; are you a cool hunter, a trend spotter, a trend forecaster or a futurist? If you are not sure of the difference between these types as well as your strong/weak points, no one will hire you. If trend forecasting is your calling, please be advised that it takes many years to become a trained, experienced and professional trend forecaster and that it requires stamina, a constant flow of clients and a strong network. Other than that, just go for it!

How important is lifestyle to fashion trends?
It is a key element in figuring out where the consumer of tomorrow is heading. Our lifestyles affect everything from what we wear, where and how we live, to what we eat and how we approach life in general.

How is the nature of trends research and forecasting changing?
The speed is increasing every year, particularly in fashion. We also work in furniture and interior where the speed is slightly slower, and in food the trends last much longer.

What are the tools no trend forecaster should be without?
Brain power and the ability to connect the dots.

What inspires you most?
Speaking to like-minded trend forecasters, futurists and creative people always brings new ideas. We hold biannual meetings in a think tank for that purpose alone. Reading both lengthy and statistical articles and reports and being overwhelmed by the sheer

amount of pictures, quotes, videos and stories online is a constant source of inspiration. The greatest sense of accomplishment is when the dots are all connected and a compelling trend story is created.

Primary vs. secondary research

Primary and secondary research can serve different purposes, but a balance of both will ensure a robust and dynamic trend.

Primary research

This is what you learn from having observed or experienced something yourself. You can conduct primary research through a range of experiences – from attending exhibitions, the theatre or cinema, or even a new restaurant, to playing with a new kind of technology. You can also attend talks, conduct interviews or take pictures. Research trips, where you look for trend ideas and material or colour inspiration in a different city or country, are another useful form of research – whether you are checking out other fashion brands, different cultural influences or just the environment itself.

Primary research, a bank of information and ideas that can be compiled for immediate or future use, helps form the seeds of an idea. This is where your intuition and experience can play a part in deciding what is new and noteworthy, what is just surfacing or exciting, and what you think may be too current or that has already worked its way into the mainstream consciousness.

Secondary research

This is what you learn from research done by other individuals or institutions, and it often takes the form of consuming different media – whether publications, broadcasts or social media – as well as other trend reports or even data. It is vital that the information gleaned is well documented in order to help with building your trend, through the collation of articles, words, interviews, screen grabs, bookmarked sites, recordings, photographs or saved imagery. Refer to the following section, 'Tracking your ideas', for more on this topic.

Secondary research can help you to elaborate on your primary ideas by giving weight to them and backing them up with other ideas from a variety of sources – demonstrating that your idea is worthy or sophisticated, as it were, and has substance behind it.

Conducting secondary research is also an opportunity to amass a strong selection of examples from a variety of different sources to back up your ideas and also to help you develop those ideas, perhaps into a new direction from the one you originally thought you were taking (see 'The art of the trend meeting', Chapter 5, pp.120–23). It is also a chance to get your body of research ready for presenting to your colleagues.

While conducting secondary research for expanding on a trend, you will also be starting to build a body of imagery that can help further along the process of creating mood boards, materials and colour ideas, which will ultimately influence product design, range building and building category collections closer to the season.

It is vital that the right balance is drawn between primary and secondary research. Too much primary research and your trend can lack robustness and appear as if it is just your opinion, while if you have too much secondary research it can feel as if your trend lacks vision, uniqueness and personality. It is also important that you do not rely too heavily on one source for your research, and that it is varied in format and origin.

To be a good forecaster, you need to be a good researcher (primary) and then an even better translator (secondary).

Personal experience

Experiencing the world around you first-hand is vital at this stage to help form the initial ideas of a trend. No trend can come purely from research. Going out to visit a gallery, exhibition, trade show or fashion show has a unique personal influence on you, and will also allow you to form your own opinions away from third-party comment or someone else's edit or taste.

Physical objects will give you a much more detailed experience of colour, materials and texture than merely reading about these things. Experiencing the placement of an object within a space as the artist would have wished it, or its actual physical use as the designer may have intended, is far more valuable than simply viewing an image in a magazine or online.

Travel is a rich source of primary research – your own experiences and observations. Artefacts from the Archaeological Museum of Heraklion, Crete.

Tracking your ideas

Once you have started to find things that interest, surprise and inspire you, you will need to find a way of keeping track of them so that these valuable ideas do not get lost or forgotten. No matter how good your memory, it is very difficult to remember all of the inspiring things you come across – so you should always track and organize your examples and ideas. There are lots of different methods you can use to do this. Detailed here are some of the most popular and effective.

Images should be sourced constantly, and filed efficiently throughout the research process. To have a broad spectrum of choice available for compiling mood boards, try to save as many relevant images as possible and also save a variety of options to illustrate a single point or product, so you have a range to choose from. Having a broad selection of images available is good practice, and saves having to re-research imagery after the initial inspiration stage.

Some trend forecasters like to use physical methods alone – such as creating folders or mood boards of images, objects and ideas – while others prefer to have a virtual storage system, using online tools or simple computer filing. Choose whichever method – or, more likely, combination of methods – suits you. And, just as we encourage you to notice things around you, you should record those things too – make notes or sketches, tear out pages from magazines, take pictures and street shots, save links or image files, or even pick up objects and papers you come across.

WHEN FILING MAGAZINE OR NEWSPAPER CUTTINGS (TEARSHEETS), MAKE A NOTE OF THEIR SOURCE AND DATE, SO THAT YOU CAN REFERENCE THEM LATER. WRITE DIRECTLY ON THE PAPER, OR ATTACH A NOTE WITH A PAPER CLIP OR STICKY NOTE IF YOU WANT TO KEEP THE IMAGE PRISTINE.

Physical tracking

Mood boards are often used as the trend-tracking method for trend
forecasting, but are not the only way to track and map your ideas.

Folders

A low-tech, but effective way to start tracking your ideas is to use folders.
These could be box files, plastic pockets or even drop files in a filing
cabinet – the format is not important. But the way you store your
precious ideas is. Starting a series of files allows you quickly to store and
organize your ideas as they crop up, and to grab or transport the ideas
whenever you need them. This method is most effective for flat objects
or articles, photo shoots and images. The best way to start is to create
basic files for different areas that you want to explore on an ongoing
basis – such as colour, silhouette and materials – or for specific
categories such as menswear, outerwear, accessories or denim. Once
you have started populating these folders, you may wish to start new
ones as you identify new patterns or trends. In this way, examples and
ideas can easily be moved from one place to another in order to keep
up with your evolving ideas.

Boards

Sticking images, objects and other research to a sheet of foam board is a well-established technique for gathering, tracking and sharing developing ideas. These boards are widely used in universities and in industry as a way to map and progress ideas, and can be especially useful when working in groups or teams as different people can add and combine references on the same board. You can also add key words, colours and objects.

Sketchbook or notebook

For many years, a simple blank book has been a creative's best friend. Whether you use it to write down ideas, or to paste inspiring objects, images and other things you find into it, a sketchbook is a great repository for ideas.

Digital tracking

It is likely that much of your research will come from online sources. Of course you can turn this digital research into physical research by printing it. But you can also use tech tools to keep track of your ideas and organize them in different ways, whether in the cloud, on your mobile device or your computer. Below are listed just some of these tools, but new apps and services are being launched all the time, so it is worth checking with tech-savvy friends and colleagues as to what they would recommend using.

Blogs

Blogs – and microblogs, such as Tumblr – can serve as a digital scrapbook for your inspiration and ideas. Many websites have 'blog this' or 'Tumblr' buttons which allow you to save articles, images and other material you like with one click. You can save each item with a few words on what interests you about it – to jog your memory later on – and even add hashtags such as #menswear or #colour to help you organize your posts. If you start to build up a lot of content, you may even find it useful to start different blogs or Tumblrs so that you can refer to your ideas more

easily. These can work like folders, so you could start a few different blogs for different categories such as materials, colour or menswear, or for different projects or seasons.

You can make the blog private, if you just want to keep your thought process and developing ideas to yourself, or make it public, which may lead other like-minded people to suggest new sources of inspiration for you.

Bookmarks/links

Bookmarks are shortcuts to online content that are stored within your Internet browser. You can easily bookmark any web page by clicking on the 'bookmark' tab or button. You can create folders for specific categories or projects, so you can find a page again more easily. Likewise, you can also keep track of things you have found online by copying and pasting their links into a document. Both of these methods offer an easy and fast way to save ideas as you go along, but remember that web pages can be moved or deleted, rendering your link obsolete.

Work in progress from University of Westminster graduates Katie Ann McGuigan (top) and Constance Blackaller (bottom).

Digital folders

You can quickly and easily save images, articles and videos in digital folders. As with physical filing, you should establish a method that allows you to find those ideas again quickly and easily.

Always find the highest-resolution version of an image that you can, and name the file in a way that will help you reference it or find it again should you need to. You should, for example, include the name of the website where you found it, or the profile name of the person who shared it on social media, as well as details of what the image is (the designer/artist/publisher/author who made it) and when it is from – this could be the date you found it or the date it was created, as appropriate. This may seem painstaking, but it only takes a few extra seconds and will enable you to find and credit the image later.

Pinterest

Tools such as Pinterest offer a simple way of gathering image-based research. As with blogs, many sites have a 'Pin it' tool, which allows you to save the image to your account in one click. You can add a few words about the source and content of the image, as well as detailing why it inspires you. The easiest way to work with Pins is to set up several boards on different themes or subjects so that you can organize and access your ideas easily, while Pinning images in a group in this way can also make it easier to spot patterns, and thereby trends.

Instagram

This mobile image-sharing network can work in a similar way to a physical sketchbook. We all take pictures with our smartphones, but you can use apps such as Instagram to save and annotate the things that interest you – whether you feature pictures you have taken yourself, or snaps of other inspiring images.

From top: Pinterest boards are a useful tool for saving themed images; USB key for Pej Gruppen trend information. Digital files can be a good way to gather research, when labelled well and kept securely.

EXERCISE: CREATE A PERSONAL TREND BLOG

Using a free platform such as Tumblr, create a blog of a trend you have spotted, using examples from multiple sources and categories. This will help you to tap into your own trend instincts.

Use a combination of content reposted from online sources as well as creating your own posts for primary research.

Try to include an example from each category listed at the beginning of this chapter. Think about:

* *What is influencing you right now.*

* *Which designers you have been following recently.*

* *Who or what is exciting you in the fashion and design industries.*

* *What new and interesting exhibitions you have seen or heard about.*

* *What in the above exhibitions resonated with you, or was memorable.*

* *Any intriguing plays, artists, performers, films or TV shows you have seen or heard about.*

* *Which new products you deem interesting.*

* *What imagery you have saved recently, and why.*

* *What kinds of subjects, people and entertainment your friends, colleagues and favourite media are talking about.*

Add notes to each example you post to your blog, in order to highlight why it is relevant to your trend. Ensure your examples include strong imagery and a diverse range of sources.

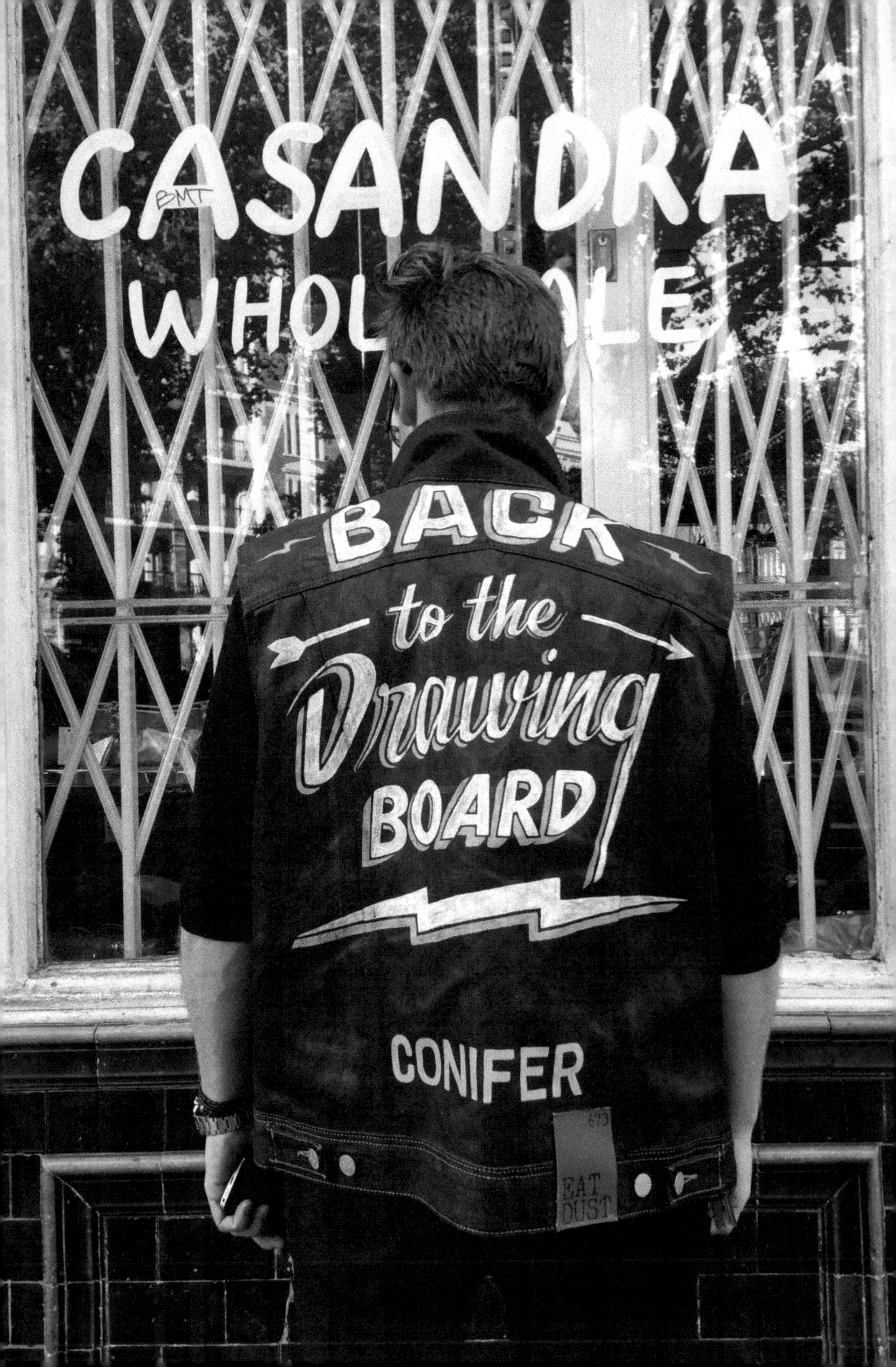
CASANDRA
BMT
BACK
to the
Drawing
BOARD
CONIFER
673
EAT
DUST

5

Trend Development

The trend process starts with conducting broad research and seeking inspiration. The next phase of creating a trend is developing your ideas to ensure they are sufficiently robust, as well as refining an idea to suit your category, market, client or consumer.

This chapter guides you through the different factors to consider when shaping your trend – refining and editing your examples, checking your ideas against the trend methodology and ensuring you are in tune with big-picture lifestyle trends, so that you are well equipped for trend meetings.

You will learn how to take your chosen research (see Chapter 4) and develop it into a strong trend idea. You will examine how lifestyle influences affect trends, how to use historical research and reference, and how to check if your ideas are worth pursuing.

The second part of the chapter offers guidance on refining your trend idea, what to expect from trend meetings and how to ensure you are working towards innovative but practical trend directions.

Observing street style can help develop trend ideas.

Developing your idea: Depth

Developing your trend begins with a wider exploration of influences, to add depth and credibility to your ideas. First, however, forecasters need to apply a series of tests to ensure their trend is definitely that – a trend.

Methodology

Trend forecasting is both art and science. While much of the trends process is about inspiration and intuition, seasoned trend forecasters use, whether consciously or unconsciously, a methodology to ensure that the trends they create are clear, forward-looking and robust.

Forecasters must understand whether trends they identify are new enough to capture consumers' interest, or realistic enough to develop into product. The checklist offered here will help refine your ideas.

'Thrice-a-trend'

There is an old truism in the trend-forecasting world (and beyond) that if you spot three examples of an idea, it is a trend. The idea works as follows:

Once = an anomaly
A single thing that stands out or piques your interest is likely to be a one-off.

Twice = a coincidence
Two similar ideas in fairly close succession are as likely to be a coincidence as the beginning of a trend.

Thrice = a trend
If you spot three distinct examples of an idea in different places or expressed in different ways, it could signify the beginning of a trend.

However, there are some caveats to this rule:

* 'Thrice-a-trend' is not a hard-and-fast rule: three examples, mixed with your own instinct, can make a broader, more complex trend that could work across a variety of time frames and product areas.

* Finding three different examples of an idea is a great way to identify a trend, but the process does not stop there. The thrice-a-trend rule is a way to test and validate your ideas – it offers a starting point for more in-depth exploration and validation, which will be explored further in this chapter.

* On social media it is easy to see three examples of an idea in the same day. To ensure that a trend is true and viable, you should see three different examples in different ways in different places – for example, on social media, in street style and at an exhibition; or you might see them on the catwalk, in pop culture and in lifestyle.

Real-world examples

For a trend to work, it needs to have a touch of reality. Can you see people around you changing the way they behave or how they dress to accommodate the trend? This is an important way to gauge if there could be a market for your trend. Some catwalk or street-style trends stay in those spheres and never cross over into the mainstream. This may be because they are too expensive, inaccessible, ridiculous or impractical for even fervent fashion fans to adopt.

Is it new?

Another key gauge for your ideas, which works in tandem with real-world examples, is asking yourself (and your team) if the idea is new enough. Just as seeing a few people adopting a new form of behaviour or way of dressing can suggest that an idea has 'legs', seeing many people adopting the idea suggests that it is no longer new (for more on this, refer to the diffusion-of-innovation diagram on p.50). And if a trend idea does not seem new at the point of research, it will certainly be behind consumer taste by the time it is translated into product 18 months later.

This is why it is important to consider who is adopting the trend, and how. You should be looking for innovators and early adopters taking interest in the idea. If you see it in the wardrobes of the majority instead, the trend is likely not new enough. If a friend who does not work in fashion already knows about it, the trend is not new enough. If the idea has already been taken on by a mainstream retailer, the notion is unlikely to be forward-looking enough to build a trend upon.

Ask yourself these questions to check the newness of your idea:
* What's new or different about it?
* What new references/elements does it include?
* Is it completely new, or a progression of something else?
* Does it excite me?
* Does anyone share my feelings?
* Can it work in my product category? Can it be translated into an actual product?

Street-shot images from outside the seasonal catwalk shows provide useful styling and product inspiration for trend forecasters.

Colour and materials trend foundations

Having started researching your trend, you now need to look at the building blocks that help you define your trend in key design terms, which are predominantly colour and materials.

Colour

Colour palettes are used alongside a trend to give a distinct mood or feeling to the trend's 'story' and to give designers a better idea of how it should be used, what sort of feeling it conveys or the market at which it is targeted.

Images can be taken from anywhere, but often include those taken from artists, photographers, exhibitions and design-led books. Personal photography, dedicated shoots or well-styled interior-design shoots may also be used as well as magazine and historical imagery.

Pinterest and Instagram can be a great source of original imagery, and are also easy to search by subject or colour. Imagery sourced for colour ideas is more object- or art-focused than other types, so that it doesn't dictate a specific product direction at this early stage.

Find your initial inspiration images and start to build a palette from there. Either use the single image that has inspired you – although one perfect image can often be hard to find – or a selection of images which pick out key colours that sum up the right feeling for your trend. Use Pantone swatches to help you build the palette, and play around with alternative colours and different layouts until you get the right combination and selection.

Materials

Material trends are led by surface and texture, with inspiration coming from physical objects rather than images. Look to interiors, material manufacturers and trade-show imagery – for example, Première Vision for materials or MAISON&OBJET for cutting-edge product design. Imagery could also come from product shots such as press or lookbook imagery, or from material libraries and archives. This part of the research is as much about the surface and its properties as the type of material it is made from, and it will ultimately be filtered down into an actual textile, or non-woven surfaces or materials as the trend progresses towards the product stage.

Put together a selection of visuals that represents the materials and surfaces that you feel are important for the season. Put them into categories – smooth, matte, compressed or contoured, for example – and then find the best imagery that summarizes each section and gives a pleasing and easily understandable visual representation.

Pantone colour swatches are matched with a styled image to illustrate how the palette works together as a whole.

Sketching footwear in the library at the Fashion Institute of Design & Merchandising, Los Angeles.

Historical research and reference

As you develop your trend ideas, it is important to include historical research and reference to add depth and clarity to your trend. As discussed in Chapter 1 (see pp.10–13), historical influences are vital to the fashion and design industries, and nearly all trends have a relationship to the past, be it a particular era, popular style or previously seen shape. Well-chosen historical examples and images can influence every part of the trend process, from colour, materials and print to macro trends, silhouette, trim and even marketing. There are many ways that these can be incorporated into a contemporary trend, depending on your product focus and the kind of trend you are creating.

Historical research and reference is a widely available and hugely inspiring source of ideas and insight. Books, art, films, architecture, interiors, textiles, exhibitions and museum archives all offer a great resource of imagery, text and ideas – not to mention the wealth of historical information that can be gleaned from the Internet.

TIP

JUST BECAUSE A REFERENCE OR EXAMPLE COMES FROM THE PAST, THAT DOESN'T MEAN IT IS AUTOMATICALLY OLD-FASHIONED. YOU CAN DISCOVER ALL KINDS OF THINGS ABOUT THE HISTORY OF FASHION AND CULTURE FROM HISTORICAL RESEARCH. FOR EXAMPLE, YOU MAY DISCOVER FORGOTTEN IMAGES OR IDEAS, OR EVEN RE-EXAMINE CULTURES, DESIGNS OR FASHIONS YOU THOUGHT YOU KNEW.

Global research

Many designers and trend forecasters take inspiration from the traditions and costume of cultures other than their own – these can also add depth and detail to your trend idea. Researching different clothing and cultures from around the world can offer useful and inspiring examples for mood, silhouette, materials, colour, print and pattern, and much more.

Historical research is vitally important to the trends process. Many collections are available to view, from current designers' work, such as the V&A's modern clothing collection (below), to visually inspiring designs from the past such as this Kibbo Kift tunic (above) at the Museum of London.

TIP

IT IS IMPORTANT TO HAVE A SOLID WORKING KNOWLEDGE OF FASHION HISTORY FOR TREND FORECASTING, AS IT IS TRUE THAT MOST IDEAS IN FASHION WILL HAVE ALREADY APPEARED IN SOME FORM IN THE PAST. FASHION FORECASTING AND FASHION HISTORY ARE NOT MUTUALLY EXCLUSIVE; IN FACT, THEY HAVE AN IMPORTANT RELATIONSHIP. HISTORY CAN HELP FORECASTERS UNDERSTAND HOW AND WHY TRENDS HAVE DEVELOPED IN THE PAST, WHICH CAN HELP THEM TO ENSURE THAT NEW TRENDS WILL BE USEFUL.

MANY PEOPLE STUDY FASHION HISTORY AS PART OF A DESIGN FOUNDATION OR UNDERGRADUATE COURSE AT UNIVERSITY. YOU CAN ALSO DISCOVER MORE ABOUT THE STYLES AND INFLUENCES OF THE PAST THROUGH LIBRARY RESEARCH AND VISITS TO HISTORICAL ARCHIVES SUCH AS THOSE AT FIT (FASHION INSTITUTE OF TECHNOLOGY) IN NEW YORK, THE VICTORIA AND ALBERT MUSEUM IN LONDON OR THE KYOTO COSTUME INSTITUTE, AS WELL AS BOOKS COVERING HISTORICAL COSTUME OR SPECIFIC ERAS IN FASHION, PLUS FASHION PHOTOGRAPHY OR FASHION HISTORY COURSES.

After initial contemporary research, you should add historical references to your mood board, blog or folders to lend factual weight to your idea and give it a grounding in the past.

Historical trends re-emerge over time and are cyclical in their influence (as discussed in Chapter 3, pp.58–59). Once a decade or era has been left behind, it may well be used as inspiration for future collections by taking the essence of a look or style from that time and repositioning it for a contemporary take – this could be a silhouette such as the 1950s New Look, a design element such as 1980s shoulder pads, or a texture such as tapestry.

Opposite: Northampton Museum houses the world's largest archive of footwear and related objects and documents, dating from the Bronze Age to the present. The collection can be viewed by appointment for research purposes.

Likewise, innovative or idiosyncratic figures from the past – such as royalty, movie stars or artists – may help to demonstrate the idea or attitude you are exploring, as well as offering historical context for a new idea.

Below: Modern and contemporary art and design are rich sources of inspiration. Barbara Hepworth's Spring 1966.

Iconic or unusual designs, objects, artworks and architecture from previous eras or design movements can also serve as useful examples of an idea. For instance, you may choose to include an image of a Barbara Hepworth sculpture to demonstrate an idea of smooth and sinuous modernity, or old scientific illustration of plants because of its unusual colours.

Industry profile
Julia Fowler

Biography
Julia Fowler is co-founder of EDITED, a retail technology company that offers real-time analytics of pricing, assortment, demand and competitive metrics to fashion brands around the world. Led by quantitative data, rather than qualitative research, EDITED helps brands and retailers have the right products at the right price, at the right time.

What was the inspiration for EDITED?
The idea came from what I felt I needed as a fashion designer, professionally. At that time my colleagues and I had internal data on the performance of previous seasons' products and access to inspirational trend books, but no understanding of the external opportunities we'd missed or concrete data on how we could improve our product assortment. As a designer, retail buyer or merchandiser, your job is to produce products that your customer wants to buy in the right quantities, sizes and price points.

Every time you see a product at a discount, it's because the wrong decisions were made somewhere along the way. This leads to a lot of wastage in the industry.

How are services like EDITED changing the way that designers, buyers, merchandisers, retailers and marketers work?
It's letting them understand their markets, their competitors and their target consumers in a completely new and effective way.

Our data primarily focuses on product assortment, pricing strategy, market performance and visual merchandising. So it's a way for brands and retailers to see how their assortments are performing against their top competitors at any time, in any category. Then, to go further and use it to help guide their decisions away from unprofitable outcomes like deep discounting or product waste.

How is the trend industry changing? What are the key drivers for fashion trends now?
Fashion trends are influenced by many factors, not just what's coming down the runway. You have influences coming from social media, retailer marketing and celebrities. More than ever, retailers need to have a 360-degree view to survive in the market.

Obviously, the story has always been that trends are changing more quickly than ever thanks to whatever new medium is out there. So right now, that's everything shared on social media where once, for example, it would have been on television. And retail has always had to keep up with that in some way. However, even the fastest retailers today aren't quick enough to be purely reactionary. There's always a lead time. Plus, virtually no brand wants to be known as a follower. As a brand you want to create the trends as often as you can, and only mimic them when you have to.

Is the industry more reliant on instant data or long-range forecasts or a balance of the two?
They're codependent, and both very vital to the success of any brand or retailer. Of course, depending on who you are, you weight them differently, but there's always a balance of both.

The kind of data we offer our users is good for both. On one hand you can analyse how things are looking in the long term, how shapes, colours or trends are declining or building up and make a confident long-term strategy based on what you're seeing. On the other hand, if you miss something you can spot that faster. You can look at the top movers week by week or day by day and react fast.

What can data-driven trend services deliver that traditional trend services can't?

It's not necessarily that data makes you predict better, but rather that it helps businesses plan for the future better and make decisions based on what the market is actually showing them. Instead of a buyer or merchandiser saying, 'Suede jackets are selling now, let's keep stocking them,' they can look and say, 'Right, how many suede jackets are on the market? How many are discounted? How have prices fluctuated in the last three months? How well did they perform last year, and the year before? Are my competitors stocking more or less of them?'

Lifestyle influences

It is important for trend forecasters to consider the changing lifestyles of their end consumer, because lifestyle influences affect fashion trends. This helps fashion brands and retailers to develop products that appeal to consumers not only in design terms but to suit the way they live.

The 'big picture'

Before the advent of global and mass-market fashion retail, most people had their clothes made by a dressmaker or tailor who knew their customers' lifestyles, or they made their own clothes. Now that the producers of fashion goods are more distant from their consumers, it is important to understand how your customers live and how their needs and wants are changing.

PESTLE analysis and lifestyle research can help with understanding shifting consumer behaviour and needs. PESTLE stands for the Political, Economic, Social, Technological, Legal and Environmental factors that can affect consumer lifestyles. It is often used as a checklist to ensure the whole picture has been considered during the trend research process.

These factors may seem a world away from fashion trends, but they shape what is happening in the world, how your consumer is thinking and, at the end of the process, what products you can actually design, produce and sell. Below is a diagram showing how relevant these business analysis factors can be to the trends industry and to the fashion industry.

Advanced Style
Older women are being addressed as important consumers. Older models such as Daphne Selfe and Iris Apfel in big demand for campaigns from Lanvin to Marks & Spencer.

Phones not Fashion
Young consumers would rather spend money on technology than on branded goods, which is having a negative effect on brands such as Abercrombie & Fitch and Tiffany. Both have redesigned their product offering.

H&M Conscious Collection
Social media pressure, and concerns about dye pollution and ethical production, helped lead H&M to launch their Conscious Collection in 2013.

PESTLE factor	Impact on the fashion industry
Political	Global trade agreements; Import and export law; Product and brand boycotts; EU, government and worldwide directives.
Economic	Recessions; Business funding; Consumer confidence; Interest rates, inflation, and other monetary policies; Spending power.
Social	The rise of celebrity culture; Popular feminism; Social media; Changing demographics; The luxury market.
Technological	3D printing; Robotic production; Materials innovation; Digital tools.
Legal	Health and safety rulings; Tax laws; Employment and competition regulations; Waste directives.
Environmental	Ethical sourcing and production; Environmental directives; Waste.

Festivals have become havens for both dressing up and for street-shot photography reports of what attendees were wearing. They have spawned a whole breed of 'festival styles' with Coachella in California leading the pack for high-street retailers' inspiration.

Lifestyle impacts trends

One of the key factors affecting trend forecasting is lifestyle, namely, how consumers' attitudes, behaviours and aspirations are changing. Festival culture is just one example of how lifestyle trends can impact fashion trends and products. Since the early 2000s, music festivals have become increasingly popular, and 'festival style' has come to dominate many summer looks in stores, in magazines and on social media. Many retailers have come to centre their high-summer collections around pieces that fit the hippie-ish or outlandish style that is so popular with festival goers.

You could trace the rise of festival culture back to influential style icon Kate Moss, who managed to look cool in jean shorts, mini dresses and wellington boots in the mud of the UK's Glastonbury Festival in 2005. Or the rise in the number of festivals around the world, from a handful of music-focused events in Europe, Asia and the Americas to events to suit every musical taste from the obscure to mainstream pop. Or consumers' desire for new and exciting experiences – festivals offer a holiday, live music and plenty of unusual experiences all in a few days. Or the increasing number of A-list celebrities who attend and perform at festivals. In fact, a combination of all of these lifestyle factors (and a few more) have led to festival style becoming a popular product category.

Data

Data is gathered and used in increasingly sophisticated ways. Many businesses, including those in the fashion industry, now rely on data to make decisions. For many years, data was considered anathema to the creative process of trend research, but it is now commonly used to support, refine and focus trends (for more on this, refer to the Julia Fowler Industry Profile, p.106). You can employ data in a variety of ways, depending on your role in the trends process.

Retail

For those working in retail roles such as buying and merchandising, sales data can offer vital insights into which styles, colours or collections are selling well and which are not. This can help inform decisions about which ranges to develop and which products to continue making or to discontinue. Market data – covering behaviour or spending across a whole category – may also influence decision making. If, for example, a certain style is selling well among competitors (say denim dresses or monk-strap shoes), then buyers and merchandisers will often want it in their own ranges, to ensure their own shoppers' needs are met. Likewise, data about the retailer's current or target consumer can influence the choice of key product areas, such as career wear or occasionwear.

Design

Trends and products developed by designers working in-house (whether in menswear, womenswear or specialist areas such as print and pattern, materials or accessories) will also be influenced by this same data, providing a framework as to how trends will be applied. Sales data, for example, may show that a particular design has been successful for several months, so designers may be encouraged to give it a new flourish with colour, silhouette or functionality.

As such, data can sometimes dictate which products you will be applying your trends to, but it can also offer opportunities – for those working in the product-design and retail areas alike. It can be used to explain why your designs will sell or why a certain colour is needed in a collection, if the data suggests it will sell well at a certain point in the year.

Market data and competitor sales can influence which pieces designers need to create in order to satisfy consumers – and are often influenced by retail teams' analyses.

Mintel data report. Data reports and quantitative analysis are used increasingly by retailers and brand strategists to help determine what products worked well and what could be done better.

Consumer/marketing

Data can also inspire your thinking in other ways – perhaps the rise of certain attitudes to technology or luxury could inform how you think about the products you create. This is especially true for roles that focus on marketing or consumer behaviours. Retailer data can help to describe how consumers are responding to products that have already been made, but consumer data – or consumer insight, as it is often described – can give more information about changing consumer behaviours that might inspire or influence new product development. A growing interest in heritage, for example, may suggest that both retail and design teams should explore a new range that takes inspiration from a brand's archives. Similarly, changing attitudes to leisure, such as a growing interest in fitness or attending festivals, would suggest that a brand needs to develop its ranges to serve those needs. Indeed, for many fast-fashion retailers, the summer music-festival season dictates the timing and design of summer ranges.

Where does the data come from?

Sales data: In-house or through specialists such as Edited and WGSN Instock.

Market data: Retail analysts such as Mintel, Forrester Research or Verdict Retail.

Consumer data: In-house consumer research, together with consumer attitudes or spending data, which can come from data specialists such as YouGov or Ipsos, or from broader research agencies such as The Boston Consulting Group or The Futures Company.

Developing your idea – refining

Once you have assembled a range of diverse and robust research – either around one theme or idea, or several different ones – you will need to refine your idea to ensure it is clear enough to share with colleagues, or even clients.

If you are creating your own trend(s), the filtering process below will help you to focus your ideas on the clearest and most compelling examples and images, before you turn them into a presentation or report (as detailed in the next chapter). If you are working with a team of other trend researchers, the filtering process helps you identify the essentials before discussing them at a trend meeting (see pp.120–23), where you will blend your ideas with others' to build the final trend directions.

Imagery

The imagery that you present (either at a trend meeting or direct to your client) should be chosen for its visual appeal and for its ability to sum up key points about the trend idea. In arranging it on a mood board or selecting images for a blog or folder, for example, check the following:

* That the colour scheme of the overall board works visually.

* That the images work harmoniously, and that none jumps out as a focal point, thereby distracting from the main messages of the trend.

* That you do not use two images where you could have used one, and that your board is not crowded.

This page and opposite: Examples of self-styled imagery used by the online trend service Unique Style Platform to illustrate their seasonal trends in both colour and surface materials.

Filtering

Filtering is a crucial process of honing your research to the right imagery and wording so that, together, it tells a clear and concise story. This makes it easier to focus the ideas and explain them to others – and, ultimately, to turn them into products.

Examples

Trend examples can be anything from article clippings and found objects to printouts, flyers, products, photographs, music or videos, books or your own photographs.

If you have several trend ideas, you should group your examples under different working titles – either through physical or digital means. Try to ensure you have examples in different formats and from different categories (as detailed in 'Primary vs. secondary research', p.88). You do not need to include all formats and categories, but ensure that you have a varied spread across each.

If you are taking your ideas to a trend meeting or collaborating with others, you should be prepared for the titles, examples and boundaries of your idea to be challenged and to change as they are further refined and tested by the group.

Filtering questions

When you are selecting images and examples to take to the next stage of the trend process, ask yourself the following:

What is most important?

Go through all the references you have pulled together for the trends and identify which examples kicked off the idea, which ones explain the idea clearly and which ones broaden it out.

Which are the newest ideas or examples?

If you have seen an idea already it is probably not new enough to include in a trend. This is because of the length of time between creating trends and the ensuing product hitting the shop floor – around 18 months (see the table on p.51). If you include an idea that is already old or mainstream at the time of creating the trend, it is very likely to be out of date by the time the product reaches stores a year and a half later.

Does it make sense to anyone else?

It can be a useful part of the trends process to discuss your trend idea with someone who is unfamiliar with it. This could be someone outside of your team or department, or even a friend or relative. If they cannot understand what you are talking about, or what ties your examples together, it is likely that your idea needs further clarification or more convincing examples.

Are my sources/references robust?

This is where all of your careful saving, naming and referencing of sources comes in useful. Ensure that you have a diverse range of examples, from both primary and secondary sources, and covering different categories, from art and music to historical references, data, pop culture and lifestyle.

If I take out one reference, does it still make sense?

Trends are made up of different things with similar characteristics – such as colour, aesthetic, mood and behaviour. The final examples within your trend idea should have several elements that cross over with other examples within your trend, to create a kind of interdependent web. If you take out one element, the others should still make sense as a trend because they have other things in common.

How could this lead to new products?

Make sure you have some initial thoughts about how your ideas might translate into products. If you cannot see how your trend could offer ideas for a new product in your category – whether that is a different style of suit or a summer sandal – then it is probably not worth pursuing as a fashion trend. These kinds of trends, however, can often form a useful framework for your ideas in the form of a macro trend.

At this point, it is important to ask yourself if the trend you are working on meets the needs of its brief – be that a specialism such as colour, a product category such as womenswear, or specific client needs. Question and discuss what your trend is about, and what you do not want it to be about. Is it, for example, a progression of something that has recently been popular – or is it something new entirely?

Targeting

Targeting is an essential part of the trends process. By working out who your trend is for and tailoring it to their needs, you are taking it from a well-researched and defined trend and making it applicable in real life.

Customer profiling is an important part of targeting a trend, and helps you to create a portrait of who the end user is and how they might use the product. A bag designer may, for example, want to see a materials forecast to help inform their leather and hardware choices, but they may also want to see the sales data for a particular region to help with their colour choices. Creating and using a customer or user profile also ensures that it reflects the needs of whoever would be using the trend – a designer, buyer or product developer, for example. This gives your trend weight, making it accessible and ultimately usable. Without this, a trend loses its utility and could end up as nothing more than a good-looking collection of references and images.

At the trend-development stage, it is also worth exploring how a key trend might play out for different brands and across a variety of markets. Ensure that you keep your user profile wide enough so that you do not target your trends too narrowly, but leave users the opportunity to translate and benefit from your trend in their own way – whether that is in their personal design style or if they are using it to fit with their own brand remit.

Filtering out who is reading a report is vital to knowing what it should contain. EDITED dress analysis dashboard.

Industry profile
Suna Hasan

Biography
Londoner Suna Hasan has designed for companies including Marks & Spencer in the UK and Esprit, Macy's and Saks 5th Avenue in the US. Moving to India in 2003, Suna was Creative Head for well-known names in the India apparel market, including Modelama Export House, Shahi Export House and Reliance Trends. As Trend Director for Stylesight, she covered the Middle East and India.

What do you do now?
I am currently working on freelance projects for the Indian market as well as my own range of luxury ceramics.

What do clients need from a trend forecast?
The Indian market is rapidly changing; clients need to understand what's going on globally. The Indian high street is transforming at great speed. Retailers such as H&M and Zara are hugely successful, and they are changing the Indian consumer's appetite for fast fashion. There has been a huge shift in the past few years in Indian shopping behaviour, which has created a larger demand for trend services. Online shopping also really took off in the last four years, making contemporary fashion accessible to smaller towns of India, which has added to the change.

Are your clients mainly manufacturers? If so, do you have to break trends down to a specific level?
Our clients at Stylesight were not only manufacturers but buying houses, export houses, fashion schools and huge retailers. Our region was India, Bangladesh, Sri Lanka, the Middle East, Dubai and South Africa. Not all segments offered by trend services are applicable to India, a warm country which celebrates different festive seasons from the global format. No consistent Indian-centric data has been offered on a regular basis by existing trend services. Yet the companies we worked with asked for Indian street fashion, collections for the festive season, Diwali for example, when people spend huge amounts of money on clothing and gifts.

Do you have a different focus for Indian clients than you would for European ones?
Totally, as India is a very traditional culture built around the family nucleus, where people marry into a family and may live with their in-laws for the rest of their lives. Certain dress codes are necessary, especially around the family at home. Western dress is fairly new to the Indian subcontinent. Indian women mainly avoid revealing clothes, super-low necks, or too much flesh showing. Jeans are the new staples with woven blouses and knitted tops. However, this is changing with millennials who are very aspirational. Dresses are emerging as a key item.

Is there a particular sector or recurring theme that Indian clients focus on?
Bollywood is a huge influence, what the popular Bollywood star wears has an enormous impact on the retail market in India.

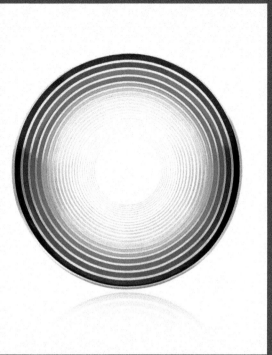

How do you approach trend research and the forecasting process?
I see what's trending, read, look, listen and observe daily life as well as researching what's happening globally.

Which sectors of the industry do you find most inspiring for your work, be they social, cultural or aesthetic?
I find the visual image the most stimulating and inspiring. Visuals have to have impact to draw a viewer in. If there is a language barrier the visuals have to be clear so the person can understand the point without having to read a lot of text.

What trend forecasting services do you use, either professionally or personally?
None, all my inspiration comes from online daily research and also seeing the world around me.

How do you think the usage of trends is changing for the fashion industry?
Everybody using trends is getting the same data and inspiration for the next few seasons, so the format doesn't encourage individuality and creative thinking in the same way.

What inspires you most?
Travel inspires me a great deal, seeing new places and cultures. Art inspires me tremendously.

What tools – website, blog, book, place, object – can you not be without?
My Mac computer, visiting my home town of London and going to Northern Cyprus, where my ancestral roots are.

How did you end up in trend forecasting?
At Première Vision I met Frank Bober, the creator behind Stylesight. I was blown away by his new development of the site, we struck up a conversation and kept in touch and the rest is history.

What advice would you give to someone who wants to get involved in forecasting?
Do an internship with a trend service first, to see if the vibe and pulse of this fast-paced industry suits their personality.

EXERCISE: CREATE A CUSTOMER PROFILE

A customer profile will help you work out who a trend is for, or what customers will be using it for. Build up an idea of who these people are: their likes and dislikes, their jobs and their professional interests as well as their personalities.

Consider these questions:

* *Who are they? Giving them a persona helps you conjure them up in your own mind – and you can use this to question your ideas as if they were a real person, as you develop your trend or as you imagine presenting it. Think about what they like and, equally importantly, what they do not. Think about what they will already have experienced, and what they might not yet have seen.*

* *What are they looking for from this trend? Are they looking for a usable design pack with colours, shapes and inspirational ideas, or are they seeking an overview of the current youth market and want to know about the latest brands, musicians or cities?*

* *How old are they? Will your trend references make sense to them, or will they need further explanation or context?*

* *How experienced are they? What is their job role? Are you talking to a junior designer or a brand CEO?*

* *What are their influences? Who do they admire, and what do they aspire to?*

* *What might be their weaknesses or strengths? Are they good at colour but less strong with materials? Are they based in New York, but want to know what is happening in Shanghai?*

Collate all your information and present it in a concise and easy-to-read manner. Use images if you find them helpful. You could even name your customer or user, and give them a gender, age, location and character profile if you think it is helpful.

Customer profiling can help to fine-tune the trends process to work out who is using it and for what.

Turning ideas into trends

Now that you have deepened and refined your research, you should have a solid trend idea that you can develop further, by yourself or with a team.

Using the methods described above, you should have a group (or several groups) of ideas united by a concept or aesthetic. You should gather these ideas together in a folder, on a blog or on a mood board to allow you to demonstrate your trend to others, and to help you decide which examples are the most compelling or innovative.

At this point, you share your ideas with colleagues in order to test and develop them further, transforming your research into distinct and useful trend directions.

Trend meetings happen at different points in the trend process. You may have meetings within your team, your category (e.g. menswear) or discipline (e.g. print) to develop your own ideas. These may then be taken to a cross-disciplinary meeting to develop overarching, or macro, trends that tie together the mood and aesthetic of the season across multiple categories and disciplines. The practices described on p.121 can be used at any kind of trend meeting.

For example, colour meetings could be held on their own as a means of developing a client-, market- or category-specific palette. The British Textile and Colour Group (and others like them around the world) brings together colour specialists from many disciplines, who create a joint palette that is presented to Intercolor, a global colour panel that offers international guidance on seasonal colour trends.

In a large fashion company or trend agency, a colour meeting may just be one part of an in-depth trend process. The colour specialists would feed into a trend meeting, along with consumer-behaviour specialists; print and pattern designers; designers of mens-, womens-, active- and childrenswear; and accessories and home-products and materials experts.

Colour palettes start off broad and are whittled down into usable ranges via a series of meetings with specialists, who all bring their own expertise and opinion. Here forecasters browse forecaster Pej Gruppen's trendstore, selling their own colour systems.

The art of the trend meeting

There are many forms of trend meeting, but in essence they all have the same aim: to bring together a range of people with different ideas and perspectives in order to build a trend. The process begins with pulling together a body of research with many cross-pollinated ideas and reference points that can then be separated and extracted into usable trends.

What to expect

Presentation

You should take both your primary and secondary research to a meeting and present your ideas, showing what sparked the initial thought – an image you found, an exhibition you visited or a street-style look you found inspirational.

   You will talk about where you got your ideas from and how you see them evolving, or about any other sources you found helpful or that backed up your idea – and then why you think the idea is important to the season, client or category.

Format

You may go 'round the room', offering everyone involved an opportunity to suggest their ideas, receive presentations from experts or present ideas in teams or groups. The initial meeting may be long – sometimes one or two days – but it will bring together many people from different specialisms. After the first meeting, you should have agreed several broad trend directions that will then be further refined by a smaller working group (see 'Types of meeting' on p.122 for more).

Application

You may also talk about which product area you could see the idea working for – women's footwear, for example. At this stage, this does not need to be as specific as a platform clog with brass-stud detailing, but it should give a general idea of where you see the idea being relevant (as part of a return to 1970s inspiration, say). Your aim should be to use words and visuals to galvanize and persuade your audience.

Trends meetings take many forms from a round-table discussion of ideas to an individual presenting their research to a larger audience.

Instinct

As we saw in Chapter 4 (see p.84), instinct and intuition play an important role in the trends process. These qualities are crucial within the trend meeting. Once each person's carefully collated research has been presented, there should always be the opportunity for people to talk about what is inspiring them personally and what gut feelings they have. More often than not these ideas will be mirrored by those of other attendees, and this can help to propel an idea existing in the back of participants' minds into the realms of a realistic trend.

Tips for effective trend meetings

* Be confident about your ideas and what you have chosen. Deliver them clearly and concisely, and do not go off subject or get distracted by others' comments.

* Be prepared to talk about your ideas in depth; suggest how each could be used, or where it could be relevant. Be clear about where it fits in the trend cycle (i.e. completely new, or a progression or amalgamation of different ideas) and where it came from.

* Eye contact, confident delivery and speaking clearly are all important when making a presentation.

* Be open to picking up on other people's ideas and improvising on the spot within a meeting. For example, someone might mention an image they like, which resonates with something you have experienced, sparking the memory of something you have seen. Be ready to add that in to your idea then and there. This strengthens and helps to build the idea.

* Open yourself up to questions, be prepared to be challenged on your ideas and fight your corner. Someone else may disagree with you or think your idea is old or irrelevant. Accept constructive criticism if you deem it valid and be prepared to drop ideas, combine them or take them in a whole new direction.

* Listen to what other people have to say as well as what people say in response to you. Their comments can be the makings of a much stronger and more usable trend.

* Lastly, check your ego at the door. You are one of many voices and opinions, and therein lies the strength of the resulting trend.

By the end of each meeting, you should have agreed three or four key trend directions, or groups of ideas. These should be forward-looking, robust, and relevant to your client or brief. You should assign a small group, or an individual, to develop these ideas further. For each trend direction, ensure you gather together the relevant examples from different members of the group for further exploration.

Types of meeting

The meeting format adopted by different companies and organizations will depend on the size of the team, the degree of internal knowledge or reliance on external expertise, how tech-savvy team members are, and whether they can easily gather in one location.

General trend meeting

This is often a round-table discussion, starting with each person presenting their ideas for the season, subject or product category. Each person will show the room their ideas and their subsequent research and findings in order to elaborate on each idea. They will present their ideas verbally and use images or mood boards to illustrate their points, discussing where they got their ideas, what they like about them and why they think they are important. Next a group – whether the whole room or possibly a smaller, core group – will edit the information and group it into similar idea categories for later development. During the whole process, note down key words that could be applied to the trend at a later stage and which will help to sum up its general mood.

The classic trend-meeting format is collaborative and exciting, and should allow people from different disciplines and experience levels to share ideas and examples – all working towards creating new trend directions.

Think tank

A think tank is a group of people who research a specific subject or a certain topic together. In trend forecasting, this might be a specialism or product area such as womenswear, denim or materials. A think tank might also work on an upcoming season, perhaps two years in advance, by starting work on the appropriate macro trends.

Generally, only specialists in a particular category or discipline attend this type of meeting. Trend meetings focusing on colour, for example, are likely to include only colour specialists.

Seminar

A seminar is a popular way for fashion professionals to get an expert, external view on trends. In this format, an expert or specialist presents knowledge and ideas to an audience. Though this is a one-way method of gaining new trend insights, it can be a useful means of gaining another view on shifts in the zeitgeist. Many companies and researchers will augment their internal trend research with external seminars to bring in new ideas, or just to check they are on the right track.

The TED Talks, run by the eponymous non-profit organization, are very popular online seminars, while Li Edelkoort is well known for her seasonal trend seminars, which set out key directions, largely based on colour and materials examples.

PechaKucha

PechaKucha translates from Japanese as 'chit-chat'; it was originally designed as an informal gathering where participants show 20 images and talk for 20 seconds on each one. It has been adopted by the trends industry as an efficient way of gleaning inspiration on a broad range of subjects quickly and efficiently. Some organizations run regular PechaKucha sessions from different specialists throughout the year, while others use them only at the beginning of a season.

Hybrid meeting

Technology has changed how we share ideas across disciplines and even across borders, meaning face-to-face meetings are nowadays not always essential. A trend meeting can include both physical and digital presence via video, Skype and social media. This method may be used if there is a core team in one location and other specialists spread across different places, and allows everyone to share and discuss ideas at the same time. This can help to expand the input into a trend beyond the organization or country involved, to include much broader influences – an especially important factor in the global fashion market.

Digital sharing

Online platforms such as blogs, Pinterest boards or even group sharing tools such as Slack can enable trend researchers to share their ideas virtually.

Digital sharing is particularly useful if you are looking for a wide range of input from different specialisms, markets and locations, as researchers can add links, images and videos remotely. It can also be useful as a way of collecting a team's ongoing research in one place, which can help streamline the trends process.

A large-scale PechaKucha trend meeting held by colour forecasters Color Marketing Group during Tokyo Designers' Week.

However, a face-to-face meeting with an individual or core team is generally required to refine and develop ideas further and take them to the presentation stage.

Conclusion of ideas

You might go through several rounds of trend meetings, or be able to conclude all of your ideas after the first meeting – this often depends on the scope of the trends you need to present.

Once you have researched, collated, developed and analysed your ideas, it is time to discard any unnecessary information and sum them up into a more concise and readable form.

Return to the filtering questions on p.114 to help you finalize your ideas, and employ the checklist below to ensure that you have the essentials before you move on to presenting them (discussed in the following chapter).

* One example of each element of the trend, with the right image for each element.

* A clear message in both idea and imagery.

* Examples from diverse sources and categories.

* Words that both explain and evoke the idea.

* Relevance to the brief.

* Relevance to the consumer's lifestyle.

* Historical references, as appropriate.

* Material, colour and print/pattern references.

* Supporting internal or external data.

* A combination of primary and secondary research.

* Agreement among your team about the focus of the trend.

EXERCISE: CONDUCT A PECHAKUCHA

Hold your own PechaKucha (see p.122), to help inspire a working trend.

Get together a group of participants, and brief them on what you would like them to do and bring. Set a time and location and, on the day, start proceedings by introducing the meeting and explaining what you hope to get out of the day. This might be a selection of influences that could inform a decision within your business, the groundwork for a new trend for a specific season, or some market research into a new product or sector.

Each participant should bring 20 slides. These could be of articles, images, exhibition listings or reviews, music, videos, books or physical objects.

Show each slide for 20 seconds, allowing each presenter that amount of time to talk about it.

Conclude the meeting with a summary of the information received and the key findings from the process. Have a number of people come up with the same idea or suggestion? Have some key themes emerged? What have you noticed throughout the meeting, and what are the other participants taking away from it?

A trend meeting in progress at Color Marketing Group, with digital and physical examples in evidence, and boards to track evolving ideas.

Nui Studio

Maxim Maximov

MATERIALER / M

Crailar / Crailar / Coloured denim
Farvet denim / Coloured denim
Mælkefibre / Milk fibers
Modal / Modal
Skifersten / Slate stone
Økologisk bomuld / Organic cotton
Hvid marmor / White marble
Ginko blade / Ginko leaves
Bambus / Bamboo
Økologisk hamp / Organic hemp
Tørret mos / Dried moss
Ruskind / Suede
Nylon / Nylon
Bomuld / Cotton
Hør / Flax
Merino uld / Merino w
Mulesing-fri uld / Mu
Sporbarhed / Trace
100 % nedbrydel
Alger / Algae
Bambusstokt
Blæk / Ink
Nanocellu
Kompres
Panar
Pike

6

Trend Presentation

This chapter looks at the many types of trend presentation and layout available. A trend is only good if it is applicable to the end user and their business. This is why your sources, images and references are key when it comes to presenting the idea. Your report will be used to explain the mood, aesthetic or product direction to other people in your team; to the wider organization; or, if you are working in an agency, to your clients. It is essential that any reader can understand the trend at a glance or on first read. All the information you have gathered should come together freely and smoothly.

Trends research is done either by a specialist team in-house or by an external agency, but both will need to explain their ideas and why they are important or applicable to the rest of the business. If each part of the business uses the same overarching macro trend, the whole business will be in line across the board, even if each department translates it differently as appropriate for its own product category.

Designers or product developers will often use a key image to inspire their design teams, so it is vital that those compiling the report pick the correct images. Other parts of a business may want to extract the research and reference parts of the report to inform marketing or visual merchandising, for example, or other relevant departments.

Trends can be presented in a variety
of formats from digital to physical,
as seen here from Pej Gruppen.

Trend titles

The naming of a trend and summing up an idea succinctly are vital in helping the trend cohere. Once you have developed your trend and are clear what it is about, you need to think of a name.

The chosen title should be easy to understand, and neither too long nor too incongruous. It should sum up the trend and give the reader a quick idea of what the trend contains and who it is for. At the same time, it is advisable to steer clear of obvious titles – such as 'Tropical' or 'Western' – that have been used many times before, and which can be misleading or vague. Try to combine an obvious notion with a word that adds a different, new dimension, such as 'Palm Shadows' or 'Future Frontier'.

These words must, of course, be connected to the trend and make sense in relation to it. The name must evoke the feeling of your trend and be easily translatable – is it masculine, floral, historic or clean, for example? Does it evoke a past era or is it futuristic? The title of your trend is aimed at anyone who might be using it or even looking at it. It is, therefore, a crucial tool for getting your user or client to understand what your trend is about and also to entice them to look further into what you have put together.

Your title must work in conjunction with the images you have chosen and not jar with anything on the page; do not, for example, use a masculine-sounding title for a women's trend (unless your trend is about gender blending, when that would be apt). Make sure that your title makes sense, and try to avoid acronyms that may need further explanation or the use of blended or portmanteau words.

Choose trend titles carefully, as they are the introduction to the trend.

Wording

It is always helpful to the reader if you supply some key words in conjunction with the naming of your trend. This could, however, depend on how much detail you are going into – a macro trend report may have more 'mood' words associated with it, while a catwalk or item trend report may include more descriptive text about detail, embellishment or silhouette.

Look through your original trend-meeting notes, and pick out key words that help to elaborate on your trend title while also summing it up. If you noted these during the presentation, discussion, development and filtering process, then this should be a fairly simple process. Try not to use too many words and make sure they are all relevant. These words could hint at the type of product you envisage your trend being used for, while still keeping the mood open to a designer or client's interpretation.

It can also be beneficial to include a short paragraph summing up what the trend is about, and perhaps explaining what all the visual elements bring to the page – whether they relate to mood, material, product or styling.

A mood board from USP. Key words and brief texts encapsulate the trend in an easy-to-grasp, straightforward manner.

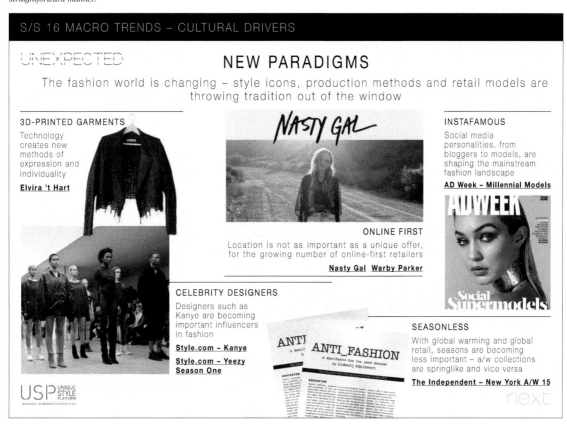

S/S 16 MACRO TRENDS – CULTURAL DRIVERS

UNEXPECTED

NEW PARADIGMS

The fashion world is changing – style icons, production methods and retail models are throwing tradition out of the window

3D-PRINTED GARMENTS

Technology creates new methods of expression and individuality

Elvira 't Hart

INSTAFAMOUS

Social media personalities, from bloggers to models, are shaping the mainstream fashion landscape

AD Week – Millennial Models

ONLINE FIRST

Location is not as important as a unique offer, for the growing number of online-first retailers

Nasty Gal Warby Parker

CELEBRITY DESIGNERS

Designers such as Kanye are becoming important influencers in fashion

Style.com – Kanye

Style.com – Yeezy Season One

ANTI_FASHION
a manifesto for the next decade
by Lidewij Edelkoort

SEASONLESS

With global warming and global retail, seasons are becoming less important – a/w collections are springlike and vice versa

The Independent – New York A/W 15

USP UNIQUE STYLE PLATFORM

next

Types of trend report

Whether you are working in a trend agency, for retail or a brand, or developing your own products, the output of a trend meeting or series of meetings is often a report or presentation, to enable you to confirm or share your ideas. Here are a few types of trend report. Reports are often tailored to a specific brand or business, so this is not an exhaustive list.

Micro
Micro trend reports are smaller, niche or fast-response reports that are specific to a subject or product and will have a direct influence for a brief time span.

Macro
Macro trends are larger, broader phenomena, which may offer inspiration that could steer the direction of the business or brand for a few years ahead. Macro trend reports often contain wide-ranging influences that could help inform the direction of a company as a whole, and can be broken down at a later date in order to inspire separate departments within the business.

Consumer
These offer a look at the consumer trends that ultimately control the commercial market across all design industries. These could include data, primary and secondary research, and they might try to define shifts in consumer behaviour.

Subject-specific
These could be trend reports on any given subject, such as retail or textiles, or can be about something as specific as an individual item of clothing for which a trend is emerging.

Timeline
This type of trend report tracks a trend from its emergence through to its adoption by key demographics and, finally, its expansion into the actual retail market and to the consumer.

Pantone® Colour Planner Autumn/ Winter 2017–18, illustrated and featuring both colour names and colour usage breakdowns.

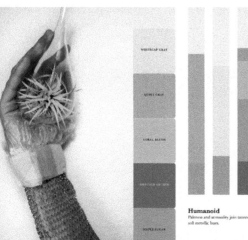

Humanoid
Paleness and sensuality join tanned tones and light, soft metallic hues.

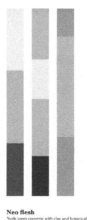

Neo flesh
Nude tones converse with clay and botanical greens to form a symbiosis between the human, the vegetal and the mineral.

GRAPHIC CITY

GRAPHIC CITY

Make-up of the trend report

Trend reports can be short and succinct or longer, resembling more of a design-direction bible for the season that could dictate all facets of a business and how they should be run or designed.

In a typical trend report, there is usually one image or a selection of images in the form of a mood board that sums it up. Then you might take that inspiration deeper into sub-reports of between three and six sections, each of which could be used to inspire different collections.

For a colour report, for example, you might take a master palette and split it into three or four sub-palettes (making sure to use your key colours for the season within them), then break it down into colour usage – as you see it being used – and smaller, product-specific palettes.

For a macro report, you would start off with a broad overview of the season and then specify three or four key trend directions, each with several subsections that group together different elements. These elements can then be used individually under the overarching theme.

For a materials report, you might create an overview and then break that down into its influences, such as surface and texture, before looking at its applicability for product and, ultimately, its use.

Print reports take colour and mood influences, then separate them into sections that can each be used to inspire print specialists.

A 'Maison' trend report from PeclersParis.

Types of presentation

*A trend presentation can take many forms; below are the most popular.
Trends can also be laid out as a book, a collage, a website, blog, video or an
infographic, to name but a few. The majority of trend presentations today
are digital, and are presented via the Internet in downloadable formats.*

Online
Trend reports can be designed in a variety of formats online to best
suit the department, brand or business at which they are aimed.
Changes can be uploaded quickly, to keep up with ever-developing
trends or to respond to new sources of information such as catwalk
analyses, news stories or trade-show reports. Digital presentations
are also instantly global, downloadable, targetable, printable and
translatable – making the Internet unbeatable as a medium for
delivering trend reports and presentations.

Social media
Social media are often used for trend presentations. Many apps and
websites lend themselves to trend reporting, with their integrated
sharing, collaboration and uploading capabilities. Pinterest and Tumblr
are the most commonly used at present, allowing users to curate their
own boards of feeds by taste, theme, style or inspiration – and to publish
them instantly, to as select or as private an audience as necessary.

Printed
Printed trend reports are the preserve of some of the more traditional
trend agencies, and are published on a seasonal or quarterly schedule,
usually with colour palettes and trend information to work alongside
them. Many businesses and designers like to have a printed trend
report, but printing is expensive and, as the report has to be prepared
some way in advance of printing, it risks being out of date as soon as it
is published.

*A swatch book of material samples
from the agency Pej Gruppen.*

Swatch books
Swatch books contain a range of physical examples, and are usually for colours or materials. Like printed reports, they are expensive to produce and once they are published they cannot be adjusted or updated.

PowerPoint
PowerPoint is the most commonly used program for seminars and trend lectures, as it is an easy tool to use for projecting to a large audience.

Trend rooms
Trend rooms are immersive physical spaces, most often used at trade shows to sum up the overall mood and trend for the show. These spaces allow visitors to look at trends and colours and to touch the fabrics, leathers or samples to get a taste of what is showing at the fair. Many trend agencies work on these spaces. Franklin Till have created spaces for Heimtextil, the annual textiles fair in Frankfurt, and Trend Selection curates the swatch, colour and trend area at the biannual leather and accessories show Lineapelle in Milan.

From top: Immersive trend room
at Heimtextil, Frankfurt, 2016;
A printed trend book from Trend Union.

Industry profile
David Shah

Biography

David Shah is the founder of Amsterdam-based View Publications, which publishes leading international trend publications including *Textile View*, *PantoneView Colour Planner* and *Viewpoint*. Shah has a background in textiles and design consultancy and gives speeches on design and consumer trends all over the world.

How has the world of trends evolved?

When I joined *Drapers Record* as the fabrics editor in around 1974 there were no trends. There were books coming out of America, but mostly people went shopping in Paris, London and Milan to buy samples you could copy. But instead of sending people all over the world to go shopping, they started commissioning reports from the likes of Here and There, David Wolfe and Doneger. This then spread to England, where Nigel French and others created trend services for clients.

A lot of the trend services started to emerge around the same time, with the new forecasters realizing that by giving clients design information and telling them what to do, what to make, they could save a lot of money by avoiding expensive mistakes. Paris had the two grandes dames of trends, Nelly Rodi and Li Edelkoort (founder of Trend Union and later editor of *View on Colour*), and they worked together to create trends.

I realized that I should be presenting trends in magazine format. I thought it was old-fashioned to just give a page in *International Textiles* (where I was editor-in-chief) to what floral a particular manufacturer was offering. Instead, I wanted to look at how everyone was doing florals and in what way. I was the first to start this in magazines, doing things from a fabric point of view, while everyone else was doing trends from a garment point of view.

Why is trend forecasting important?

Nobody can work without a map, and whether that's an Ordnance Survey paper map (like the physical trend books and mood boards) or Google maps (like digital trend services and online tracking) people still need maps. The route and the destination is up to you, but you still need a map.

How important is lifestyle to fashion trends?

Lifestyle has always been important for fashion trends. In the 1980s there were some big films that were hugely influential. *Out of Africa*, for example, started huge trends because of the leads in their safari jackets; everyone was going around in khakis.

We all start with the consumer now, not the product. That's why watching lifestyle is so important. For example, the athleisure trend is not about being able to wear the same clothes to the gym and to dinner – it's about making things easier for yourself, and at the same time making your clothes more functional.

What kinds of presentation are most effective?

People still want stories, but they want practical market information too. Trend stories are still relevant, but clients also need to know what is hot and new, which might not be a trend but a key item. They also need to know the market demand – the commercial, practical element – and understand the changing lifestyle of their target customer.

We need trends because while people always need to see the big picture, trends work on many levels now. It's not just about predicting big waves of ideas – it's also about spotting things that are new and could be very commercial.

PANTONE® VIEW

Colour Planner

AUTUMN | WINTER 2017-18

WOMENSWEAR MENSWEAR ACTIVEWEAR COSMETICS INTERIORS INDUSTRY GRAPHICS

What do clients need from a trend forecast?
The future of the trend business is inspiring and confirming – clients want both of those things. You could create the most inspirational presentations or books, but ultimately, the client wants to know if they should do black or white. Trend directions are no longer just information, they're about helping brands and retailers know how to apply that information.

What advice would you give to someone starting out in trends now?
Intuition is important, but you should read the *Financial Times* too, because the world is about money and spotting opportunities.

EXERCISE: MAKE A SIX-PAGE TREND PRESENTATION

Find a theme and work it into a full trend presentation of a maximum of six pages. Take inspiration from something you feel is emerging, and research around that theme. Ask yourself: Where is this trend coming from? Where is this trend now? Where is this trend going?

Aim for an overview of your trend and its inspiration. Think how you can provide information to sum it up, and make it relevant and applicable to the reader. Put forward fresh ideas that are inspiring to the reader. The presentation should be self-explanatory as a whole trend pack, and it can be either physical or digital.

Here is a suggested layout guide, and some points to bear in mind when compiling your presentation.

Page 1: Mood board
* Use relevant primary and secondary imagery for your mood boards.

* Add depth to your trend with physical swatches and contemporary inspirations.

* Include a colour palette – name the colours if you feel this adds to the overall mood.

* Choose a suitable trend title; you may want to add some mood words, too.

Page 2: Research and reference
* Write up six to eight research references, influences and cultural drivers clearly and concisely, making sure that all are relevant. They should merit around 50 words each, and each have a single image.

* If your presentation is digital, make sure that any video links are correctly embedded.

Page 3: Materials and detail
* Show a selection of materials that inspire this trend, and a range of details that could be useful to the reader.

* In a physical presentation, consider including real materials or trims if they are relevant.

* Digital presentations could include scanned swatches alongside a selection of images.

Page 4: Print and pattern
* Provide a page of print or pattern influences for the trend.

* Choose a range of images that could take the trend in a variety of directions, and inspire readers or designers in different ways.

Pages 5 and 6: Styling and product
* Choose suitable imagery, or supply your own product drawings, to suggest how the mood, materials and pattern would translate into your chosen product area(s).

* Supply styling images for your chosen trend to show how it would play out from the mood into product, how the look would work as a whole and with what other products.

Spend some time on the design and layout (see pp.137–39 for tips). Make sure the whole presentation is cohesively designed and makes sense from start to finish.

Design and layout

The design of your trend report is crucial not only to how it looks but also how it is perceived by the reader. To make sure your trend is used to its full potential, bear the following points in mind when thinking about or designing the content and format of a trend presentation.

* Images are a crucial part of any trend report, and we have discussed in previous chapters the importance of choosing the right imagery. Having spent so much time researching, selecting and editing your images, they should be used for maximum impact.

* Images should be cropped to remove any unnecessary background or colour. Make sure the reader focuses on exactly what you intend.

* Images should be balanced within a mood board. Avoid grouping similar images together, and ensure the colours work well as a whole.

* Present the elements neatly, with the same distance between images on every page. Choose your font sizes and styles carefully and keep your design uniform throughout.

* Think about the audience viewing your presentation or the reader using it, and let them dictate its style. Should it be casual, formal or highly professional?

A product design and surface trend report from Viewpoint *magazine.*

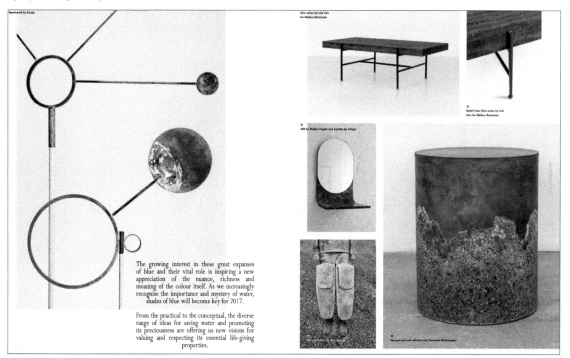

* Think about the design of your presentation or report. Could each page work on its own for a different team, so the report could be split up if necessary?

* If this is an online trend, are you ensuring that people can add to it constantly, so that it can evolve?

* Is this a 'big splash' trend to impress people and show you know what you are talking about? If so, make sure that the design backs that up, the imagery is arresting and your references are absolutely right.

* If it is to be printed and distributed widely, make sure the design works well on an A4 page. Decide if it should be portrait or landscape and stick to one format.

* If the report is just for one or two people, consider including physical material swatches or actual samples.

* If the trend is technology-focused, does the report need to include video? If so, make sure that the links and images are properly embedded and play correctly on all formats.

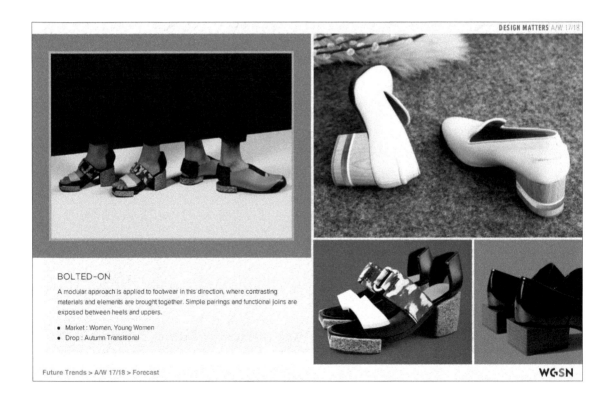

DESIGN MATTERS A/W 17/18

BOLTED-ON

A modular approach is applied to footwear in this direction, where contrasting materials and elements are brought together. Simple pairings and functional joins are exposed between heels and uppers.

• Market : Women, Young Women
• Drop : Autumn Transitional

Future Trends > A/W 17/18 > Forecast

WGSN

A footwear product and design detail trend overview from WGSN.

CONTEXT

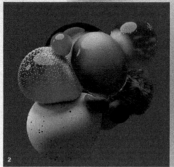

PSYCHOTROPICAL EXPLORES AN IDEALISED NATURE OF THE FUTURE.

In 2018, we will seek out not just the natural, but the super-natural, either through eco-tropical paradises or manmade wonderlands. Environments will become 'phygital' hybrids – hyper-textured, hyper-exotic, and hyper-sensorial – and our focus will shift towards experiences, as well as innovative materials and technologies that create feelings of euphoria and soft psychedelia. This is escapism at its best, as we seek out and celebrate the more sensual side of the world around us.

WGSN

FUTURE TRENDS CRITICAL PATH S/S 18

THE VISION ■
MID-MAY

COLOUR ■

Active Colour Analysis
LATE-MAY

Active Colour
LATE MAY

Global Colour
EARLY JUNE

Colour Analysis
EARLY JUNE

Colour Evolution
EARLY JUNE

Regional Colour Comparison
MID-JUNE

Colour by Region
MID-JUNE

Beauty Colour Cosmetics
MID AUGUST

Kids' Colour
LATE JULY

Men's Colour
LATE JUNE

Lifestyle & Interiors Colour
MID-JULY

Women's Colour
MID-JULY

Accessories &
Footwear Core Colour
EARLY AUGUST

FORECAST ■

Surface & Materials
Forecast
EARLY JUNE

Men's Textiles Forecast
LATE AUGUST

Women's Textiles Forecast
MID AUGUST

Active Textiles Forecast
EARLY SEPTEMBER

Kids' Textiles Forecast
LATE SEPTEMBER

Big Ideas
LATE JULY

Active Big Ideas
EARLY JULY

Packaging Forecast
LATE SEPTEMBER

Accessories & Footwear
Hardware & Details
MID AUGUST

Performance Footwear
Forecast: Textiles & Surface
MID AUGUST

Women's Forecast
LATE JULY

Lifestyle & Interiors Forecast
LATE JULY

Men's Forecast
MID-JULY

Kids' Forecast
LATE AUGUST

Active Forecast
EARLY JULY

Knit & Jersey Forecast
LATE JULY

Accessories & Footwear
Leather & Non-Leather
EARLY AUGUST

Accessories & Footwear
Solid Materials
EARLY AUGUST

Visual Merchandising
Forecast
MID-DECEMBER

Women's Denim Forecast
EARLY SEPTEMBER

Men's Denim Forecast
EARLY SEPTEMBER

Accessories Forecast
MID TO LATE SEPTEMBER

Footwear Forecast
LATE SEPTEMBER TO EARLY OCTOBER

Jewellery Forecast
EARLY SEPTEMBER

Intimates Forecast
MID-DECEMBER

Swimwear Forecast
LATE SEPTEMBER

Prints & Graphics
Design Capsules
EARLY SEPTEMBER

KEY ITEMS ■
LATE JULY TO LATE SEPTEMBER

DESIGN DEVELOPMENT ■
EARLY TO LATE SEPTEMBER

WGSN

From top: Page from WGSN seasonal trend report; Schedule of trend reports published by WGSN to help clients know when to expect key information.

There are advantages and disadvantages to both physical and digital presentations, and each has its place. There are no hard-and-fast rules, and it is up to you to decide which format you choose – or you may have both in one presentation. Online trend reports and presentations must be downloadable so that they can be saved and stored and, above all, be printable for the reader. A team manager will often distribute them, and make notes on them or highlight important sections that must be noted or adhered to.

7

Trends in Practice

This chapter explores what happens next, after you have researched, refined, concluded and presented your trend idea: the real-world outputs of trend forecasters' ideas. We look at who uses trend information and the practical application of trends to different companies, markets and sectors. We also highlight the interplay between fashion and other lifestyle industries, examining how the same trend may play out across a number of categories.

Once a trend is completed and presented – to the client, your team, or to another area of your business – it takes on another life. Your audience or client will take the trend you have defined, and will translate that into their product area using their own expertise. This could take many forms, from informing what products should be bought to inspiring the look of a retail environment or creating a style-and-design guide to inform a team of designers what they should be creating and how their product should look.

Fashion companies are not the only businesses using fashion forecasts. Many leading tech, design, consumer-goods, transport, automotive and other companies use fashion forecasts to inspire new thinking in their category, and to ensure they are ahead of the needs of their consumer. After all, fashion consumers do not only buy fashion – and the depth of analysis conducted by the trends industry can help to signpost changing attitudes in other areas.

Designer Hussein Chalayan's Autumn/Winter 2000 collection, including the 'coffee table dress', blurred the lines between fashion and product design.

How companies use trends

Companies use trends differently; the same trend is often translated in different ways across the market by a number of companies. How they apply this to their product can vary wildly, depending on how individual designers translate that trend, how relevant the trend is to that company and what they think will sell well in their market. Price point, target-customer profile, retail format and brand image can also impact on how a trend is translated.

Frayed denim

No doubt inspired by the resurgence of 1990s style in the 2010s, a handful of brands started to produce denim-led collections, changing the 'denim landscape'. London-based designers Marques'Almeida played a key part in this by making the frayed hem a fundamental part of their look. This caught on over time and they went on to produce a more accessible denim collection in collaboration with Topshop, which pushed the trend into the mass market. Many brands have taken the original style and reworked it in a variety of ways, all using the same simple trend detail. The latest move for the look sees the high-fashion brand Vetements, a Parisian 'design collective', taking vintage denim and reworking it into clever panels and misaligned shapes, and coining the phrase 'Vetement hems' for a feature that has now also been copied by the mass market.

Clockwise from top: Graduation show by Marta Marques and Paulo Almeida from Central Saint Martins, 2011; Outside Ferragamo fashion show, Milan Men's Fashion Week, 2016; Vetements, Autumn/ Winter 2014; Sandals by New Look, 2016.

Opposite, clockwise from top left: Musicians First Aid Kit, 2014; Coachella, 2016; Laura Ashley wedding dresses, 1986; Philosophy di Lorenzo Serafini, Milan Fashion Week, Spring/Summer 2016.

Prairie

The Prairie look has been intermittently popular since it was a genuine fashion style in the 1870s. In the 1970s, the television series *Little House on the Prairie* (set in the 1870s) brought the look back into popular consciousness. Many high-fashion brands seized on it for inspiration, since it fitted perfectly into the flowing feminine and floral look of the time. UK-based label Laura Ashley built its business on Prairie style during the 1970s and 80s. The Prairie look has since been in and out of fashion. The Swedish sisters Klara and Johanna Söderberg, from the band First Aid Kit, rejuvenated the look in 2013, and it has also been seen on many catwalks over the last few decades – from Philosophy to Chloé. It has also appeared in many high-street brands after its appearance as a key look at the annual Coachella festival.

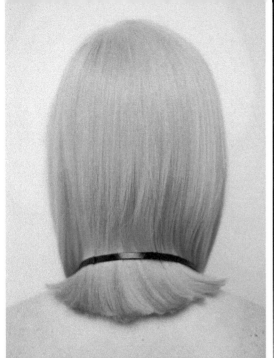

*Clockwise from top left: Ally
Capellino lookbook image, from her
Spring/Summer 2015 collection
in partnership with the Glasshouse
Salon, Hackney; Pink coat by
Simone Rocha, Autumn/Winter 2013;
Kanye West showing Yeezy Season
2, New York Fashion Week, Spring/
Summer 2016.*

How trends are applied across multiple products and sectors

In our Instagram- and Pinterest-ready consumer world, images of products and trends can spread incredibly fast, allowing manufacturers and designers to pick up on trends easily and quickly. This has led to the proliferation of trends across many sectors; the same trend often appears in many forms. Below are two examples of a trend spreading from one brand or category into a much wider arena.

The first is the colour pastel pink, which since 2010 has spread from hair products to coats and accessories across many levels of the market. So prevalent has pastel pink become that it was used by Kanye West as a neutral colour in his second Yeezy collection in 2015, demonstrating how the trend emerged into the mainstream before evolving into a new and more exclusive form.

The second trend is marble, which started as a sculpture and furniture trend first seen at the Milan Furniture Fair and was appropriated into fashion, footwear, technology and back into interiors (albeit mainly as a print) over the following few years.

Clockwise from left: Jil Sander Menswear Autumn/Winter 2008; iPhone 6 case by Native Union, made of real marble; KUFcakes by KUFstudios (artist: Kia Utzon-Frank). The cakes are covered in marble-printed marzipan, 2016; Nails by Nailed by Grace, Grace Humphries.

Industry profile
Helen Job

Biography

Helen began her career as a music and fashion journalist and worked at WGSN when it was the only major trend forecaster. Moving to New York, she taught trend forecasting and consulting for a number of big agencies and brands, including the Flamingo Youth network. She is now Head of Cultural Intelligence at Flamingo.

How do you approach trend research and the forecasting process?

I have been working in this industry for well over a decade and my approach has changed considerably. I began reporting on and 'trendspotting' in the field, travelling with a camera, street shooting at festivals and clubs. It was more about cultural immersion. Now the idea that you could predict a change in the street fashion of Stockholm by looking at what is happening in Tokyo has gone, as everything is happening simultaneously and the info is widely shared.

My career has transitioned. What I do now is more akin to cultural analysis – absorbing masses of information, scouring for subtle shifts in the cultural landscape and identifying white spaces of opportunity for my clients. I see my role now less as a trend forecaster and more as a trend translator and facilitator of change.

Do you have a methodology?

I am always interested in new methodologies and combining methodologies to develop the most appropriate research plan for a client and then experimenting with output. It's vital that the work we produce is really useful and can be embedded into client thinking and planning, and internal and external strategy.

In most cases we begin with an 'as is' assessment: where does the client currently sit in the cultural landscape? Who are their competitors? These could be across category, for example are teens spending less on clothes and more on caffè lattes? What fears and ambitions do they have for their brand? Then I can come up with a set of provocations and hypotheses about what is happening and the direction of change. I then stress-test these hypotheses, speaking with experts and instigators to see if my hunches are correct.

During this process I am able to see opportunities – where the trend directions identified are going to produce either an area that is neglected by brands or where there is a growing consumer need (even if they don't realize it yet) and a brand could step in with a solution or product.

Which sectors of the industry do you find most inspiring for your work, be they social, cultural or aesthetic?

I have spent the bulk of my career working in the youth market and it is still what excites me the most. I am obsessed by unearthing subcultures and new music, and the publications and artefacts that come out of these various scenes. I think it's because – particularly with leading-edge youth influencers – this is the fastest-moving sector and where many mainstream trends originate.

What trend forecasting services do you use, either professionally or personally?

I don't subscribe to any services but I read a lot of newsletters and attend industry talks out of interest and to sense-check some of my thinking. I always read Protein and attend The Future Laboratory Trend Briefing. I'm all for a trend commune – a sharing of ideas makes us all better at serving our clients' needs, and I love to work collaboratively on projects with other research and creative agencies.

How do you think the usage of trends is changing for the fashion industry?

I think the desire from clients is for more tailored, bespoke end-to-end research. All the big agencies now offer an advisory service. When there is so much free information, fashion brands really need to understand 'what does

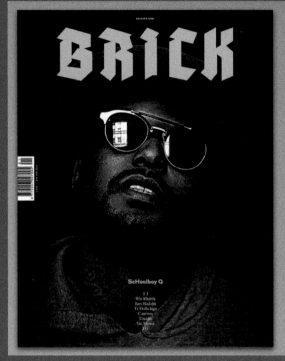

*BRICK, a music and lifestyle
publication representing new
hip-hop culture and one of Helen
Job's sources of inspiration.*

this mean for me?' and most importantly 'how do I stay competitive in such a crowded marketplace?' I also think the idea of predicting 24 months in advance and thinking seasonally is dying, if not already dead. Change is so rapid now, it is difficult to predict and keep pace. It is better to focus on really great product and understand the ever-changing context in which your product is viewed, and facilitate the culture in which your consumers live.

What inspires you most?
It's a trite answer but people and places. Nothing makes me happier or more excited than immersing myself in a new city or neighbourhood and engaging in conversation with fantastic brains. I love learning new things. I guess that's why I'm still working in this industry.

What tools – website, blog, book, place, objects – can you not be without?
Slack and Airtable! The biggest challenge in my day is organizing the multitude of thoughts buzzing around my head. These apps have changed everything. Slack allows me to order my thoughts and links by theme and Airtable keeps track of all my projects and expert contacts.

Beyond that I love magazines – browsing through bookstores in any city is a favourite activity and stumbling across new youth titles feels like a luxury. And of course you need a nice-looking notebook and pen, preferably from Japan!

Please describe your current job role and explain how trends play a part in it.
I head the Cultural Intelligence team at Flamingo, an international research agency with a brilliant and varied client list. In Cultural Intelligence we track the shifts, trends and ideas shaping the future, to help businesses and brands take advantage of change. We identify social and cultural tensions that rub against each other to detect ripples of cultural change. We don't call ourselves trend forecasters, but by observing these shifts you can begin to predict the direction of change.

From a personal point of view I also keep an eye on trends within our industry to ensure our offer feels fresh and exciting to our clients. Working in this industry it's imperative to keep innovating and make sure you are embodying the trends you are preaching.

How do lifestyle trends play out in the fashion arena?

There has always been a strong symbiosis between fashion and lifestyle trends, becoming ever closer in recent years. Brand collaborations are one manifestation, with brands from different sectors coming together. Brands enter into collaborations with those from which they wish to gain credibility and an inroad into a new market; both sides seek potential advantages from sharing their consumer base.

Make-up brand Face Stockholm have collaborated with Reebok to create limited-edition footwear collections in 2015 and 2016. Meanwhile, Barbour joined forces with Land Rover in 2014 – the former borrowing 'cool' from a brand, and the latter confirming a dependable image by association. For more on the interplay between fashion, culture and lifestyle, refer to Chapter 4.

This page: Barbour for Land Rover, Autumn/Winter 2015.

Opposite, clockwise from top left: 1967 dress by Paco Rabanne, made of lightweight metal squares held together by metal links; A prototype of a futuristic stereo (never produced), designed by Lester Beall in 1959; A scene from the film 2001: A Space Odyssey, 1968.

The space race

Consumers' fascination with new technologies and pastimes has long influenced fashion trends. The dream of space travel was realized in 1957 by the Russian spacecraft Sputnik, and popularized even further when US astronaut John Glenn orbited the earth in 1962. This influenced much of global pop culture at the time, from TV shows, toys and product design to architecture, movies and transportation – and fashion was certainly not immune to this trend.

In high-shine metallics and plastics, with minimal, geometric silhouettes, designers such as André Courrèges, Pierre Cardin, Paco Rabanne and Rudi Gernreich translated the fascination with space travel into high fashion. These designs looked protective, technical and futuristic, which perfectly suited the innovative, anti-establishment mood that permeated much of the 1960s. Courrèges' first space-inspired collection launched in 1964, and this adventurous, progressive ideal was translated into futuristic fashion trends that continued throughout the mid-1960s.

Athleisure

One of the most visible examples of lifestyle trends impacting fashion in recent years is 'athleisure'. As people become more interested in well-being, and certain exercise brands such as SoulCycle and CrossFit have gained attention, trend forecasters observed an impact on fashion trends. They saw that people were more keen than ever to show off their active lifestyles, and so were wearing activewear at all times of the day, not just pre- and post-exercise. This led to a rise in niche brands, such as Lucas Hugh and Outdoor Voices, who created design-led activewear to enable consumers to wear fashionable clothing in their leisure time, too. This trend became a hugely desirable category, with higher design expectations from consumers leading retailers at all levels, from Net-a-Sporter to H&M, to introduce athleisure product.

EXERCISE:
TRACK A TREND

Take a trend that you can see emerging, and track its evolution across a variety of markets and sectors. You can either track a trend that has emerged from fashion and moved into other lifestyle categories or track a trend that has spread into fashion from elsewhere.

You could include examples from interiors, leisure, travel and transportation, health and beauty, technology, and food and beverages.

Ask yourself the following questions:

* Where did it originate?

* How is it being applied to a range of products?

* Has it changed sector since it first emerged – for example, has it changed from a fashion trend to a beauty one?

* Does applying this trend to new products make it more appealing to a wider audience?

* Where do you see it going next?

* Do you see this as an emerging trend, a fad or a classic (see p.53)?

* Why do you think it has managed to span many product sectors?

Present a range of images from each category, from the emergence of the trend, its evolution and mainstreaming. Back them up with a selection of research and reference examples.

Opposite left to right: Lucas Hugh 2016; H&M For Every Victory sports collection, launched July 2016, was developed in collaboration with the Swedish Olympic team.

Above: Onzie, Fall 2016 collection.

Conclusion

Fashion trend forecasting is a creative practice with a real commercial outcome. If you can balance the inspiration elements – new ideas, curiosity and creative thinking – with the reality of thorough research, targeting customers and their lifestyles, and identifying product needs, you can create robust, exciting trends that reduce risk for retailers and brands and spark creative products that consumers will love.

We talk about trend forecasting as being an art and a science. It requires imagination and ingenuity as much as careful analysis and thorough research. By understanding how the zeitgeist is changing and what trends develop as a result of this, you will be well equipped to create and sell new products, and gain an invaluable insight into how the world is changing.

We hope that the insights, exercises and tips in this book will help you to create well-considered trends that lead to ever newer and more interesting fashion products. The trends process takes time, practice and experience. We hope we have given you the skills and encouragement to try it for yourself.

Discussing a moodboard at Stylus.

Glossary

athleisure activewear worn at any time of day, not just during exercise

baby boomer cohort born after World War II, when the birth rate spiked. Baby boomers are now at retirement age

banner advert an ad embedded into a web page

Belle Epoque period of settled and comfortable life preceding World War I

brand worth often used in the marketing industry to describe the added value a brand name brings to a company's products and assets; also known as brand equity

bubble up the theory that the aesthetic of niche groups, styles and subcultures bubbles up from the underground to influence mainstream trends (also known as trickle up theory)

CADs (from computer-aided design) graphics used in trend reports and presentations

category collection a designed collection centred round one specific category type such as swimwear

CEO Chief Executive Officer; often the highest-ranking person in a company

celebrity stylist a fashion stylist who creates outfits for celebrities to wear at public appearances

chemise à la reine (French) light muslin sashed dress, popularized by Marie Antoinette

churidar (Hindi) tight trousers worn by people from South Asia

classic style a trend with mass appeal that lasts for a generation or more, for example the trench coat or jeans

colour cards samples of colours originally produced by French textile mills (which dictated what was popular in Paris, and as a result in America), distributed to US manufacturers and retailers

colourway any of a range of combinations of colours in which a style or design is available

comp shopping comparisons conducted by retailers into how key trends are being used by their competitors

consumer insight/consumer data information about shifts in consumers' tastes and aspirations, used in the forming of future trends

diffusion-of-innovation theory theory proposed by Everett Rogers, describing how trends spread from a few innovators to reach a peak with the 'late majority' and then die down

ennui dissatisfaction

e-tailer online retailer

exoskeleton a gaming suit that provides a player with varying responses based on their position, speed of movement, and other sensed data

fad very short-lived trend

fashion plate an illustration showing or advertising new fashions; widely used before colour photography

fashion stylist someone who creates looks for photographic shoots, for advertising and editorial uses

fast fashion copying trends from the catwalk for the high street, to hit global stores in just a few weeks, thanks to smart production models

flapper style a 1920s trend among fashionable young women; the flapper dress had no waistline, allowing greater freedom of movement than earlier fashions

gender neutral applicable to males or females; in fashion, garments that could be worn by either gender

Georgian period the years 1714–1830, during which Britain was ruled by Kings George I–IV

Grand Tour a cultural tour of Europe undertaken in the eighteenth century by upper-class young men as a part of their education

kurta (Persian/Urdu) loose, collarless shirt worn by people from South Asia

lookbook a collection of photographs compiled to show off a model, a photographer, a style – or a stylist or clothing line

macaronis (from Grand Tour + eating macaroni) young men of the mid-eighteenth century whose extravagant modes of dress were adapted from foreign fashions

macro trends lifestyle trends, dependent on entertainment, culture, food, technology and design

microblog a blog site designed specifically for short posts, which could be text, images, or videos. Examples are Twitter, Tumblr and Pinterest

millennials cohort born after 1980 and reaching adulthood in the early years of this century; sometimes known as Generation Y

mood board an assembly of images, materials and pieces of text, to evoke a particular style or concept

New Look style popularized by Christian Dior after World War II and characterized by long gathered skirts and defined waistlines

overlasted platforms a platform shoe with the upper stretched over (a device to make high heels more wearable without the obvious look of a platform)

pattern grading a way of sizing a pattern up (or sometimes down) while maintaining the proportions of the original

PESTLE acronym for the Political, Economic, Social, Technological, Legal and Environmental factors that can affect consumer lifestyles

portmanteau word one combining the sounds and meanings of two others, e.g. 'motel' (motor + hotel), 'brunch' (breakfast + lunch)

PR (public relations) both a person whose job it is to garner publicity for brands they represent, for example by persuading journalists to feature products in magazines, and the job itself

product life cycle the rise and fall of a product, and by extension of a trend

range building expanding a selection of products that all work together in a theme

salwar (Persian/Urdu) trousers

silhouette the basic outline of clothing on the body

smart data analysed, filtered data that is targeted to a specific need or goal

smart production a form of manufacturing that utilizes advanced information and cutting-edge technologies

street report the collation of street style images into easily understandable groups and visual trends

streetshot informal style of photography, often unposed and spontaneous, taken in the street

style tribes groups of people united by a distinctive look, and often seen as different from the mainstream

sumptuary law a law limiting or forbidding personal expenditure; often applied to modes of dress

talons rouges (French) red-heeled shoes restricted to the upper classes by Louis XIV

tearsheets magazine or newspaper cuttings

trend cycle the way in which trends fade and return across a span of decades, typically a generation

trend reporting a way of describing the current market by looking at retailers, sales data and consumer media

trend rooms physical immersive spaces that give the user an experience of, and feeling for, the trends they are conveying

trend tracking real-time monitoring of current products; in fashion, this would include colours, materials and silhouettes

trickle across the theory that trends are available at all levels of the market simultaneously (in contrast to both trickle down and bubble up)

trickle down the theory that trends adopted by those at the top of the social order trickle down various market levels to influence what those at the bottom will wear

trickle up *see* bubble up

trunk show an event at which vendors present merchandise directly to store personnel or customers at a retail location or another venue (such as a hotel room) before it is made available to the public

visual merchandiser someone who designs displays for shop windows and shop floors, and may also determine store layout

zeitgeist (German) spirit of the age

Key trade shows

Bread & Butter, Berlin
Fashion
Biannual
www.breadandbutter.com

Consumer Technology Association (CES), Las Vegas
Technology
Annual
www.ces.tech

Heimtextil, Frankfurt
Materials
Annual
heimtextil.messefrankfurt.com

Lineapelle, Milan
Leather
Biannual
www.lineapelle-fair.it

Maison&Objet, Paris, Singapore, Miami
Interiors
Annual
www.maison-objet.com

Milan Furniture Fair, Milan, Moscow, Shanghai
Interiors
Annual
www.salonemilano.it

Pitti Filati, Florence
Materials
Biannual
www.pittimmagine.com

Pitti Uomo, Florence
Menswear
Biannual
www.pittimmagine.com

Premiere Classe, Paris
Accessories
Biannual
www.premiere-classe.com

Première Vision, Paris
Textiles
Biannual
www.premierevision.com

Key events

The Armory Show, New York City
Arts
Annual
www.thearmoryshow.com

ArtBasel, Basel, Miami Beach, Hong Kong
Arts
Annual
www.artbasel.com

Cannes Film Festival, Cannes, France
Film
www.festival-cannes.com

Dutch Design Week, Eindhoven, Netherlands
Design
Annual
www.ddw.nl

Frieze, London, New York
Arts
Annual
frieze.com

London Design Festival, London
Design
Annual
www.londondesignfestival.com

South x Southwest (SXSW), Austin, Texas
Technology, marketing
and entertainment –
Annual
https://www.sxsw.com/

Sundance Film Festival, Park City, Utah
Film
Annual
www.sundance.org/festival

Venice Biennale, Venice
Arts
Biennial
www.labiennale.org

Further reading

Brannon, E L and Divita, L R. *Fashion Forecasting*, 4th edition (2015), Fairchild Books

Cassidy, D and T. *Colour Forecasting* (2005), Blackwell Publishing

Kim, E, Fiore, A M, and Kim, H. *Fashion Trends: Analysis & Forecasting* (2011), Berg

McKelvey, K and Munslow, J. *Fashion Forecasting* (2008), Wiley-Blackwell

Polhemus, T. *Street Style* (2010), Pymca

Raymond, M. *The Trend Forecaster's Handbook* (2010), Laurence King Publishing

Rousso, C. *Fashion Forward: A Guide to Fashion Forecasting* (2012), Fairchild Books

Scully, K and Johnston Cobb, D. *Colour Forecasting for Fashion* (2012), Laurence King Publishing

Sims, J. *100 Ideas that Changed Street Style* (2014), Laurence King Publishing

Index

Page numbers in **bold** refer to pictures

Picture credits

The publishers would like to thank the following for their help and contribution to this book.
a = above, b = below, l = left, r = right

Pages 2, 6 Unique Style Platform; 8 Transcendental Graphics/Getty Images; 11al Ray Stevenson/REX Shutterstock; 11ar Retna/Photoshot; 11b IPC Magazines/Picture Post/Getty Images; 12a Walker Art Gallery, Liverpool/Wikimedia Commons; 12b Tim Rooke/REX/Shutterstock; 13 Louvre Museum, Paris/Wikimedia Commons; 15al Virginia Turbett/Redferns/Getty Images; 15ar Guildhall Library & Art Gallery/Heritage Images/Getty Images; 15b Miguel Juarez/The Washington Post/Getty Images; 15c Burton Berinsky/The LIFE Images Collection/Getty Images; 16a buzzfuss/123RF.com; 16bl Everett Collection/REX/Shutterstock; 16r Ebet Roberts/Redferns/Getty Images; 17a Han Myung-Gu/WireImage/Getty Images; 17b Private Collection/Bridgeman Images; 18 Bravo/NBCU Photo Bank via Getty Images; 19 Moviestore Collection/Alamy; 20l ACME Imagery/Museum of Fine Arts, Boston/SuperStock; 20r Stefano Tinti/123RF.com; 21l Roger-Viollet/REX/Shutterstock; 21r John Twine/Daily Mail/REX/Shutterstock; 23al WGSN; 23ar Fashion Institute of Technology – SUNY, FIT Library Special Collections and College Archive; 23b, 26 Peclers Paris; 24 Color Association of the United States; 28 Pej Gruppen; 29 Martin Beureau/AFP/Getty Images; 30 Buckitt, photo Alan Burles; 33 Christian Vierig/Getty Images; 34 Pinterest, Inc; 34 www.quartermastertrends.com, @quartermastertrends; 40, 41 © Stylus Media Group 2016; 42, 43 courtesy Ingrid de Vlieger; 44 Amy Leverton, photo Sadia Rafique; 45 Amy Leverton, photographed at Evan Kinori, San Francisco; 47 Scout; 48 courtesy Yasemin Cakli, @yaz_menswear/photo Simon Armstrong; 52 Justin Tallis/AFP/Getty Images; 54l Startraks Photo/REX/Shutterstock; 54r Bob Daemmrich/Alamy Stock Photo; 56 www.view-publications.com; 57 Alex Segre/REX/Shutterstock; 60 Dave M Benett/Getty Images for Burberry; 61 Mustafa Yalcin/Anadolu Agency/Getty Images; 62 Charles Sykes/REX/Shutterstock; 63 Jeremy Sutton-Hibbert/Alamy Stock Photo; 64 Melodie Jeng/Getty Images; 66 courtesy Aki Choklat, photo Ruggero Mengoni; 67 courtesy Aki Choklat. À Paris by The Style Council © Polydor Records, 1983, photography Peter Anderson; 68 Timur Emek/Getty Images; 70 photo Giulia Hetherington, with thanks to Magma, London WC2; 72 Giulia Hetherington; 73 Venturelli/Getty Images for Gucci; 74 Victor Virgile/Gamma-Rapho via Getty Images; 75 Julien Boudet/BFA/REX/Shutterstock; 76 Rosie Sparks/House of Hackney; 77 Salone del Mobile, Milano, photo Saver Lombardi Vallauri; 78 Peabody Essex Museum, Salem, Massachusetts, photo Walter Silver; 79l Jim Dyson/Getty Images; 79r Cyrus Kabiru in collaboration with Amunga Eshuchi, Big Cat, C-Stunners Photography Series, courtesy Ed Cross Fine Art; 81 UsTwo.com; 82l Heimtextil/Frankfurt Messe/Pietro Sutera; 82r Unique Style Platform; 83 Chris Saunders, courtesy PAPA Photographic Archival and Preservation Association, Kapstadt/Cape Town; 84 WeWork.com; 86, 87 Pej Gruppen; 89l & r Rae Jones; 91 courtesy Isabel Brooke, instagram @sapelbr; 93a courtesy Katie Ann McGuigan, www.katiemcguigan.com, instagram @k_a_mcguigan; 93b courtesy Constance Blackaller, www.constanceblackaller.com, instagram @ceblackaller; 94a Bloomicon/Shutterstock; 94b Pej Gruppen; 96 Amy Leverton, hand-painted denim by Ornamental Conifer; 99 DSerov/Shutterstock; 101 Unique Style Platform/© Pantone LLC, 2017; 102 courtesy Fashion Design Institute of Design & Merchandising, Los Angeles; 103a © The Estate of John Hargrave/Museum of London; 103b Victoria and Albert Museum, London; 104 Northampton Museum and Art Gallery; 105 Peter Macdiarmid/Getty Images for The Hepworth Wakefield; 106, 107, 113 EDITED; 109 STS/wenn.com; 111 Mintel Group; 112, 113 Unique Style Platform; 116a & b courtesy Suna Hasan; 117 courtesy Suna Hasan. Tableware from the Solar Collection by Suna Hasan; 118 martiapunts/Shutterstock; 119, 120, 126, 128 Pej Gruppen; 123 PechaKucha, photo Michael Holmes; 124 Color Marketing Group; 129 Unique Style Platform; 130 from Pantone® View Colour Planner A/W 2017-18, www.view-publications.com; 131 Peclers Paris; 132 Pej Gruppen; 133a Heimtextil/Frankfurt Messe/Pietro Sutera; 133b Fred Causse for Trend Union; 134, 135, 137 www.view-publications.com; 138, 139a & b WGSN; 140 Steve Wood/REX/Shutterstock; 142 Tinxi/Shutterstock; 142a Marques'Almeida, marquesalmeida.com; 142bc Vetements, photo Oliver Hadlee Pearch, vetementswebsite.com; 142bl New Look, newlook.com; 143al photo Neil Krug/Sony BMG/Wikimedia Commons; 143ar WGSN; 143b Laura Ashley; 143c Anton Oparin/123RF.com; 144al photo Agnes Lloyd Platt for Ally Capellino; 144ar Eamonn McCormack/Getty Images; 144b Randy Brooke/Getty Images for Kanye West Yeezy; 145ac Native Union; 145l Olycom SPA/REX/Shutterstock; 145ar Kia Utzon Frank, photo Owen Silverwood; 145br Grace Humphries, @nailedbygrace, nailedbygrace.tumblr.com; 146 courtesy Helen Job; 147l BRICK magazine, @brickthemag, brickthemagazine.com, photo of ScHoolboy Q by Alexandra Leese; 147r BRICK magazine, photo of Wiz Khalifa by Neil Bedford; 148 Land Rover; 149al UPPA/Photoshot; 149ar Bettman/Getty Images; 149b Archive Photos/Metro-Goldwyn-Mayer/Getty Images; 150 H&M Hennes & Mauritz, hm.com; 150 Lucas Hugh, LucasHugh.com; 151 Onzie, @onzie, www.onzie.com; 153 © Stylus Media Group 2016.